英語総合教材

THE LIVES AND TIMES OF MOVIE STARS

映画スターの人生と活躍の日々 -再改訂版-

編著者
寶壺貴之 ‖ Craig Alan Volker

共　著
井土康仁 ‖ 中澤大貴 ‖ 山田優奈

スクリーンプレイ

THE LIVES AND TIMES OF MOVIE STARS

© Copyright 2013

by

Screenplay Dept. of FOURIN, INC.

本書にはドットコードが印刷されています

リーディング力とリスニング力がつく
音声ペン "iPen" システム

【ドットコードとは？】

　グリッドマーク株式会社が開発し、特許を所有する「ドットコード音声データ再生技術」のことです。通常の文字印刷に加えて、パターン化された微小な黒い点の集合体（ドットコード）を印刷する一種の「二色刷り」のことです。

　本書では、次ページにご案内してある本文英文ページに施されています。ルーペなど拡大鏡で見ると目視できます。

【ドットコードはどう使うの？】

　スクリーンプレイでは、本書に関連した「音声データ」と音が出るペン "iPen" （ともに別売）を発売しております。

　ドットコード印刷された部分に "iPen" のペン先を当てると、"iPen" のスキャナーがドットコードを読み取り、内蔵された micro SD メモリ内の「音声データ」とリンクしてペンから音声が聴こえるシステムです。"iPen" のさらに詳しい説明は、スクリーンプレイのホームページをご覧下さい。

https://www.screenplay.jp/

　本書での、具体的な使い方は、128頁と129頁をご覧下さい。

音声ペン "iPen"

お近くの書店へご注文されるか、下記まで直接ご連絡ください。

スクリーンプレイ

☎ 052-789-1255

<本書の取り扱いについて>

■ 本書のドット印刷されている箇所に鉛筆、油性ペンなどで文字や絵を書いたり、シールなどを貼ったり、消しゴムでこすったりしないでください。"iPen" が正常にドットコードを読み込まなくなる恐れがあります。

■ 水など液体にご注意ください。濡れたり、汚れたりすると不良の原因となります。

■ 購入時に正常だった書籍が、後に、ドットコード異常になった場合、返品やお取り替えの対象となりませんのでご了承ください。

<音声再生上のご注意>

■ 紙面にペン先を当てる際は、確認音声が終わるまでしっかりと "iPen" に読み込ませてください。読み込み時間が十分でない、または適切な使用方法でない場合、再生音声が途切れるなど動作不良の原因となります。

<おことわり>

■ 本書のドット印刷部分以外に "iPen" のペン先を当てても音声は再生されません。

■ スクリーンプレイ発売「音声データ」以外や不正に入手された「音声データ」で "iPen" をご利用になられると "iPen" 本体ならびに「音声データ」の故障の原因となります。当社は一切の責任を負いかねますのでご了承ください。

ドット印刷箇所

● 本書は、各章冒頭の *Introductory Conversation* と *Reading Passage* のすべてにドット印刷されています。語句解説と *Exercise* には印刷されていません。

は　し　が　き

　現代のグローバル化が進む世界の中で、英語学習におけるコミュニケーション重視の方向性は益々顕著であり、日本でも「『英語が使える日本人』の育成のための戦略構想」が謳われるなど英語教育は重要な時期を迎えています。英語を学習する上で最も適した題材とは何でしょうか。おそらく「映画」はその問いの答えのひとつになります。英語の映画を日本語や英語の字幕を付けて見る、または字幕を付けないで見るといった英語学習の方法は、日本でも比較的ポピュラーになりつつあります。

　英語の映画を見ることが学習に役に立つ理由は2つあります。1つ目は、ネイティブ同士の英会話を聞くことによって現代英語の文脈で学習することが可能です。ネイティブスピーカーが使っている言語を生で学べる「映画」という手段は、言語として英語を学ぶ上で役に立つことは間違いないでしょう。2つ目は、学習にエンターテインメント性が付加されるといった点です。英語を学習する際、SVO だとか SVOC だとかの文法を学ぶのは避けられませんが、映画であれば人々を惹きつける、楽しませるために練られたストーリーがあなたを魅了しながら学習をさせてくれるはずです。

　さて、英語学習の手段として映画を用いるメリットは分かっていただけたところで本書について触れます。上述したように、ある特定の映画を取り上げてそれを題材にした映画英語教材は多々ある中で、本書はアメリカハリウッド映画の中でも特に有名な俳優を30人取り上げて、その俳優自身に焦点を当てて彼ら彼女らの歩んできた道を題材とし

た英語学習者向けの教材です。多くの映画にはストーリーに登場するキャラクターを演じる俳優が存在します。そこで、本書は有名な映画に登場する俳優を切り口に、彼ら彼女らが出演した映画の情報や人生を中心とした文章を執筆し、それを基に数多くの問題を作成しました。

　各章では、最初に俳優が出演した映画の中でのワンシーン等の写真があります。その写真を見ながら Introductory Conversation として簡単な英会話を学習します。次に Reading Passage としてその俳優に関する文章を読みます。文章理解の手助けとして語句解説もしてあります。そしてエクササイズについては、T-F Quiz 、Japanese to English 、Structure and Vocabulary と多くの問題を解くことで総合的に英語力向上を目指します。

　本書を通して、映画俳優の知識と英語の基礎的な能力を養い、映画での英語学習の土台としていただくことを願っています。また、映画俳優の人生についても学習していただける内容になっていますので、その人となりも理解していただきその後に好きな俳優の出演映画をご覧になっていただければ幸いです。なお、本書の内容は、岐阜聖徳学園大学短期大学部平成24年度研究助成金「映画を利用した効果的な英語学習－登場人物と映画台詞に焦点を置いた学習－」（寶壺貴之）の研究成果の一部であることを付記させていただきます。

　最後に、本書の出版に際して、この企画に賛同いただき発行にご尽力いただいた、株式会社フォーインの鈴木雅夫社長と、いつも的確で丁寧な編集作業をしてくださったスクリーンプレイ編集長の鈴木誠氏に、この場を借りて感謝いたします。

2013年4月　　　　　　　　　　　　　　　　　　　　著者一同

［参考文献］

『ジーニアス英和辞典』	第4版	（大修館書店，2006年）
『新和英大辞典』	第5版	（研究社，2003年）
『新英和大辞典』	第6版	（研究社，2006年）
『広辞苑』	第6版	（岩波書店，2008年）
『プログレッシブ英和中辞典』	第5版	（小学館，2012年）
『ロングマン現代英英辞典』	5訂版	（桐原書店，2008年）

────────── **Exercise の構成** ──────────

Exercise 1 : T-F Questions
Exercise 2 : Japanese to English
Exercise 3 : Structure and Vocabulary

Exercise 1（True-False Questions）
　　正誤問題は本文の内容を十分に理解していれば正解できるように工夫しています。文章をよく読み、リーディング力が向上するようにも工夫しています。

Exercise 2（Japanese to English）
　　基本的な英作文の問題を設定しましたが、会話文・本文にある英語表現を十分に理解していることによって、その表現を応用すれば書けるように工夫しています。

Exercise 3（Structure and Vocabulary）
　　4択問題です。本文の内容を十分に理解していれば、出題文の意味を容易に類推することができるように出題してあります。また、基本的で比較的使用頻度の高いイディオムや単語、熟語を選んで復習できるように配慮してあります。

【語句解説】
　　語句解説欄は特に難解と思われる単語や熟語、固有名詞、人名、組織名、歴史上の出来事などを解説しています。
　　小さな数字は、解説語句のある『行』を意味しています。

Contents

1. **Drew Barrymore** ·············· 8
   ドリュー・バリモア

2. **Ingrid Bergman** ·············· 12
   イングリッド・バーグマン

3. **Jack Black** ·············· 16
   ジャック・ブラック

4. **Abigail Breslin** ·············· 20
   アビゲイル・ブレスリン

5. **Nicolas Cage** ·············· 24
   ニコラス・ケイジ

6. **Kevin Costner** ·············· 28
   ケビン・コスナー

7. **Russell Crowe** ·············· 32
   ラッセル・クロウ

8. **Michael J. Fox** ·············· 36
   マイケル・J・フォックス

9. **Mark Hamil** ·············· 40
   マーク・ハミル

10. **Tom Hanks** ·············· 44
    トム・ハンクス

11. **Anne Hathaway** ·············· 48
    アン・ハサウェイ

12. **Audrey Hepburn** ·············· 52
    オードリー・ヘップバーン

13. **Harrison Ford** ·············· 56
    ハリソン・フォード

14. **Whitney Houston** ·············· 60
    ホイットニー・ヒューストン

15. **Samuel L. Jackson** ·············· 64
    サミュエル・L・ジャクソン

16. **Nicole Kidman** ·············· 68
    ニコール・キッドマン

17. **Youki Kudoh** ·············· 72
    工藤夕貴

18. **Jennifer Lopez** ·············· 76
    ジェニファー・ロペス

19. **Marilyn Monroe** ·············· 80
    マリリン・モンロー

20. **Paul Newman** ·············· 84
    ポール・ニューマン

21. **Brad Pitt** ·············· 88
    ブラッド・ピット

22. **Keanu Reeves** ·············· 92
    キアヌ・リーブス

23. **Julia Roberts** ·············· 96
    ジュリア・ロバーツ

24. **Arnold Schwarzenegger** ··· 100
    アーノルド・シュワルツェネッガー

25. **Will Smith** ·············· 104
    ウィル・スミス

26. **Sylvester Stallone** ·········· 108
    シルベスター・スタローン

27. **Sharon Stone** ·············· 112
    シャロン・ストーン

28. **Ken Takakura** ·············· 116
    高倉健

29. **Robin Williams** ·········· 120
    ロビン・ウィリアムズ

30. **Bruce Willis** ·············· 124
    ブルース・ウィリス

THE LIVES AND TIMES OF MOVIE STARS

★1★
Drew Barrymore

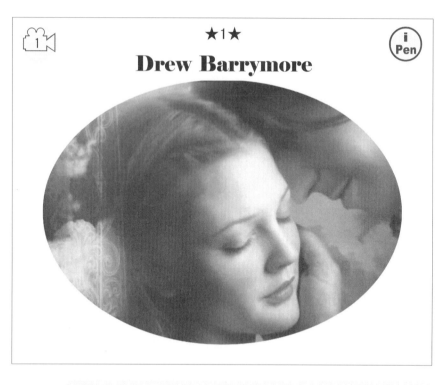

Yumi :Ricky, I haven't seen your friend Toshi lately. Is he still around?
Ricky :Sorry, didn't I tell you? He's off in Kenya.
Yumi :Kenya? What's he doing in Africa? Lucky him, he's always going off on cool holidays.
Ricky :Not a holiday. His company gave him six months to work with the UN World Food Program. They're delivering trucks to deliver food to Somalia. He asked to look after the trucks when they arrive. They're new models and they needed a Japanese mechanic to show people how to keep them in good shape.

Drew Blyth Barrymore was born in 1975 into a family of American actors. She made her first appearance in an advertisement when she was only 11 months old and her first movie appearance when she was only 5 years old (in *Altered States*). She had a difficult time growing up. She wrote about her successful struggle to overcome teenage drug and alcohol problems in her autobiography *Little Girl Lost*.

She has been in many movies and is a part-owner of her own film production company. One of her most famous movies was *Ever After*, which won many awards when it was released in 1998. Besides her acting work, she is also active in problems of the Third World. She was named the United Nations World Food Program Ambassador Against Hunger and has given over a million dollars of her own money to it. In recent years she has become interested in photography, which is becoming more and more important to her. She and her fiance Will Kopelman gave birth to their first child in 2012.

---

p8→₁ **lately**：最近　₁ **be around**：周りにいる　₃ **be off**：休暇をとっている　₃ **Kenya**：ケニア・アフリカ東部の国で首都は Nairobi　₆ **company**：会社　₇ **the UN**：国際連合・1945年設立で、本部は New York 市にある　₇ **World Food Program**：国際連合世界食糧計画は、食糧の乏しい国への援助と被災国に対して援助を行い、社会や経済の開発を促進する国際連合の機関である　₈ **deliver**：届ける　₈ **Somalia**：ソマリア・アフリカ東部の共和国で首都は Mogadishu　₉ **look after**：～の世話をする

p9→　₂ **appearance**：出現　₃ **advertisement**：広告　₆ **struggle**：奮闘　₆ **overcome**：克服する　₇ **autobiography**：自叙伝　₁₂ **release**：公開する、封切する　₁₂ **besides**：～するだけでなく　₁₃ **the Third World**：第三世界・アジア・アフリカ・中南米などの発展途上国のこと　₁₄ **ambassador**：大使　₁₈ **Will Kopelman**：ウィル・コペルマン・美術コンサルタントでドリュー・バリモアの夫

THE LIVES AND TIMES OF MOVIE STARS

♥ Exercise 1-1 ♥
TF Quiz

以下の文章が本文の内容と合っていれば T 、誤りなら F を記入しなさい。

( ) 1. Drew Barrymore was born into a family of American actors in the twentieth century.

( ) 2. She started her actress career when she was 11 months old.

( ) 3. *Little Girl Lost* is her autobiography.

( ) 4. One of her most famous movies was *Little Girl Lost* which was about her successful struggle to overcome teenage drug and alcohol problems.

( ) 5. In addition to her acting work, she is also active in problems of the Third World.

♥ Exercise 1-2 ♥
Japanese to English

以下の日本語の文章を英語に直しなさい。

一週間、ジャッキーはニューヨークで休暇を過ごしている。

_____

英語を教えるだけでなく、彼は舞台俳優もやっている。

_____

Drew Barrymore

♥ Exercise 1-3 ♥
Structure and Vocabulary

次の空欄に文脈に即した単語を下記から選び記入しなさい。本文の内容が
ヒントになるものもあります。

1. One of her most famous movies was *Ever After*, which
    (   ) many awards when it was released in 1998.

    (A) gets

    (B) gotten

    (C) get

    (D) got

2. (   ) being capable, she had good luck.

    (A) But

    (B) Except for

    (C) Besides

    (D) Then

3. It's so hard to (   ) the problem of starvation in
    third world countries.

    (A) try

    (B) encourage

    (C) invest

    (D) solve

- 11 -

★2★
Ingrid Bergman

Yumi :That was a good movie, but I don't know if I understood why it was set there in Casablanca. Why were all those people from Europe there in Morocco?

Ricky :Ah, aren't you glad you're with someone who studied history? Before the 1950s, Casablanca was a neutral city. That meant it didn't take part in any war. It was separate from any other country. So people wanting to get to a free country went there and waited until they could get enough money and the right papers to leave for a safe country.

Yumi :Oh, I see. Thanks, Mr. History Student.

Ingrid Bergman

Ingrid Bergman was born in Sweden in 1915 to a German mother who died when she was three years old and a Swedish father who died when she was thirteen. Her acting career began when she won a competition for a scholarship with the Swedish Royal Dramatic Theater, where she studied drama. She acted in a play after only three months and left after a year to start acting in movies.

She came to the United States in 1939 to act in a movie, but was unable to speak any English. By 1942, when she played a lead role in *Casablanca,* her English was fluent. During her career she acted in Swedish, English, German, Italian and French. She is often described as the world's most international actress. She was in many highly successful films and won many awards.

She died in 1982 because of breast cancer. Several years before she died, she wrote an autobiography. In it she talked very openly about her childhood, her marriages, and her very colorful romances.

---

p12→　2 **set**:設定する　　2 **Casablanca**：カサブランカ・モロッコ北西部の港市
4 **Morocco**：モロッコ・アフリカ北西部のイスラム教王国で首都は Rabat　6 **history**：歴史　6 **neutral**：中立の　7 **take part in**：〜に参加する　8 **separate from**：〜分かれる
9 **free country**：自由が保障された国
p13→　1 **Sweden**：スウェーデン・北欧の王国で首都は Stockholm　　4 **competition**：競争、コンテスト　5 **scholarship**：奨学金　5 **the Swedish Royal Dramatic Theater**：スウェーデン王立演劇場　7 **acting**：俳優業　8 **the United States**：米国・50の州と District of Columbia（一つの首都地区）から成る北米連邦共和国　9 **be unable to**：〜することができない　10 **play a lead role**：主役を演じる　11 **career**：経歴　12 **be described as**：〜として表現される　　14 **award**：選考の結果に対して与えられる賞
15 **because of**：〜のために　15 **breast cancer**：乳がん　18 **colorful**：華やかな

- 13 -

THE LIVES AND TIMES OF MOVIE STARS

♥ Exercise 2-1 ♥
TF Quiz

以下の文章が本文の内容と合っていれば T 、誤りなら F を記入しなさい。

( ) 1. Ingrid Bergman was born in Sweden in 1915 to a German mother who died when she was three years old and a Swedish father who died when she was thirteen.

( ) 2. In 1928, her Swedish father was dead.

( ) 3. Though she could not speak English, she moved to the United States in 1939.

( ) 4. She died in 1982 because of lung cancer.

( ) 5. In her biography, she talked about her childhood, her marriages, and her colorful romances.

♥ Exercise 2-2 ♥
Japanese to English

以下の日本語の文章を英語に直しなさい。

映画『アルゴ』の舞台はイランである。

_____

彼女はスペイン語を流暢に話し、ポルトガル語も少しわかる。

_____

- 14 -

Ingrid Bergman

♥ Exercise 2-3 ♥
Structure and Vocabulary

次の空欄に文脈に即した単語を下記から選び記入しなさい。本文の内容が
ヒントになるものもあります。

1. The recent increase in people who suffer from lung
    cancer has raised concerns (   ) smoking.

    (A) regard
    (B) regards
    (C) regarding
    (D) regarded

2. Her acting career began when she won a competition for
    a (   ) with the Swedish Royal Dramatic Theater.

    (A) fee
    (B) scholarship
    (C) fare
    (D) rate

3. (   ) just a few years, her English skill has
    become very sophisticated.

    (A) With
    (B) On
    (C) In
    (D) At

- 15 -

★3★
Jack Black

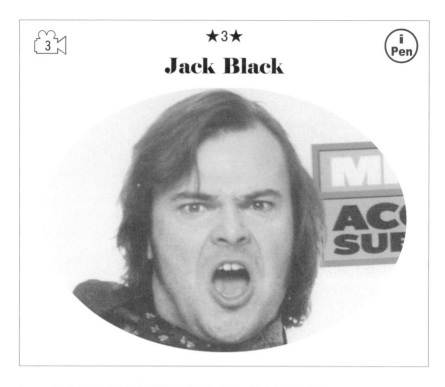

Yumi : Did you have to take music at school?
Ricky : Yeah, in elementary school. But I kept up with music classes in high school, even though we didn't have to take them.
Yumi : Oh yeah? I don't see you as much of a classical music guy.
Ricky : I'm not. I chose rock music. We learned about the history of rock and pop music and how it all began. We had to make bands and perform. I played the keyboard.
Yumi : You could take rock music in school? Real *School of Rock*! Wow, that's a lot different from my high school!

Thomas Jacob Black was born in 1969 in California. His parents were rocket scientists. From an early age he was nicknamed "Jack." Although he was in a video game commercial as a teenager, his acting career did not really start until he was a university student and got roles in television shows. He quit university after two years to try to act full-time. His father stopped supporting him after this.

From television he was able to get into small movie roles. His role in *School of Rock* was especially popular. Most of his roles have been in comedies. He often plays sloppy immature young men who try everything to succeed. He often starts a part speaking slowly and quietly and then switching to singing more and more loudly and quickly.

He is the lead singer in Tenacious D, a comedy rock band that has released two albums. He has also sung with other groups.

He is married to his high school girlfriend. After high school they had not seen each other for fifteen years. They met by accident and got married a year later. They now have two sons.

---

p16→ ₂**elementary school**：小学校　₅**classical music**：クラシック音楽　₇**rock music**：ロックンロールから派生したロック音楽　₈**pop music**：popular music の略語で歌謡曲、流行歌　₉**perform**：演奏する　₁₂**different from**：〜とは異なった
p17→ ₁**California**：カリフォルニア州・米国太平洋岸の州で州都は Sacramento　₂**rocket scientist**：ロケット工学者　₃**video game**：テレビゲーム　₄**teenager**：十代　₅**university**：大学　₇**support**：扶養する　₉**role**：役割　₁₀**comedy**：喜劇　₁₀**sloppy**：だらしない　₁₁**immature**：大人げない　₁₄**lead singer**：leading singer の略語で主旋律を担当し、コーラスを先導する歌手　₁₅**release**：レコード・本などを販売する　₁₉**by accident**：偶然に

THE LIVES AND TIMES OF MOVIE STARS

♥ Exercise 3-1 ♥
TF Quiz

以下の文章が本文の内容と合っていれば T、誤りなら F を記入しなさい。

( ) 1. Thomas Jacob Black was born in 1969. His parents were actors.

( ) 2. Although he was in a video game commercial as a teenager, his acting career did not really start until he was a university student and got roles in television shows.

( ) 3. One of the most popular movie roles was in *School of Rock*.

( ) 4. He often plays sloppy immature young men who try everything to succeed.

( ) 5. He is married to his college girlfriend.

♥ Exercise 3-2 ♥
Japanese to English

以下の日本語の文章を英語に直しなさい。

今年、火曜日の午前に代数とフランス語を取っている。

_____

翌月、あのグループは新しいアルバムを発表する。

_____

- 18 -

Jack Black

♥ Exercise 3-3 ♥
Structure and Vocabulary

次の空欄に文脈に即した単語を下記から選び記入しなさい。本文の内容が
ヒントになるものもあります。

1. He (   ) university after two years to try to act full-time.

　　(A) leave

　　(B) leaving

　　(C) leaven

　　(D) left

2. Due to the explosive growth of the space engineering departments, the government needs (   ) rocket scientists.

　　(A) most

　　(B) more

　　(C) meet

　　(D) must

3. They met (   ) and got married a year later. They now have two sons.

　　(A) until

　　(B) sometimes

　　(C) absolutely

　　(D) by chance

★4★
Abigail Breslin

Yumi :Ricky, if you got a million dollars, would you keep on working or would you just enjoy life?
Ricky :I guess I would probably do something. I mean, I would quit my job waiting on tables for sure. But I think I would want to do something. Maybe work with my sister's charity or something. I mean, you have to do something. You can't just sit around all day. What about you?
Yumi :Me, too. I think I would use the money to go back to university and study to be a veterinarian. Then I would open up a free animal clinic.
Ricky :That's sounds like a great idea. There are many sick pets these days, but vet bills are expensive.

Abigail Kathleen Breslin was born in New York City in
1996. Her first acting role was in a toy store television
commercial when she was three years old. Three years later
she got her first acting role in a successful science fiction
movie with Mel Gibson.

After that she was in several movies, but her first really
big success was in *Little Miss Sunshine*, a comedy about a
family who drive together across the United States so their
young daughter can be in a beauty contest. For this role she
was nominated for an Academy Award. She was the
youngest actor ever nominated for an Academy Award.

Since then she has continued to be in other successful
movies. In recent years she has also played in a rock band,
"CABB." She says that if she stops acting when she is older,
she would like to become a veterinarian or fashion designer.
She may not need to worry about work though; she is one of
Hollywood's richest young actors, earning more than a
million dollars in 2006 alone.

---

p20→ ₁ **a million dollars**：100万ドル　₃ **probably**：多分　₄ **quit**：やめる　₄ **for
sure**：確かに　₇ **have to**：～しなければならない　₈ **What about you?**：あなたは
どうですか　₉ **go back to**：～へ戻る　₁₁ **open up**：(商売などを) 始める　₁₁ **free**：
無料の　₁₁ **animal clinic**：動物診療所

p21→ ₂ **toy store**：おもちゃ屋　₂ **television commercial**：テレビのコマーシャル
₄ **science fiction**：空想科学小説・SF　₅ **Mel Gibson**：メル・ギブソン・アメリカ合衆
国ニューヨーク州ピークスキル生まれ映画俳優、映画監督である　₇ **comedy**：喜劇
₉ **daughter**：娘　₉ **beauty contest**：美人コンテスト　₁₁ **nominate**：ノミネートする
₁₃ **in recent years**：近年では　₁₃ **rock band**：ロックバンド　₁₅ **veterinarian**：獣医
₁₅ **fashion designer**：ファッションデザイナー　₁₆ **worry about**：～について心配する
₁₇ **rich**：金持ちの　₁₇ **earn**：お金を稼ぐ　₁₇ **more than**：～以上　₁₈ **alone**：だけで

THE LIVES AND TIMES OF MOVIE STARS

♥ Exercise 4-1 ♥
TF Quiz

以下の文章が本文の内容と合っていれば T 、誤りなら F を記入しなさい。

(　　) 1. Abigail Breslin was born in the late 20th century.

(　　) 2. She got her first acting role in a science fiction movie at the age of three.

(　　) 3. She was nominated for an Academy Award for the role she acted in the movie called *Little Miss Sunshine*.

(　　) 4. Since her future dream is to become a veterinarian or fashion designer, she is eager to quit her job immediately.

(　　) 5. It is said that she earned more than a million dollars in 2006.

♥ Exercise 4-2 ♥
Japanese to English

以下の日本語の文章を英語に直しなさい。

もし今、大きな病気にかかったら、重大な経済的な問題を抱えるだろう。

_____

私たちはその賞の候補に挙げられたが、他の人が受賞した。

_____

Abigail Breslin

♥ Exercise 4-3 ♥
Structure and Vocabulary

次の空欄に文脈に即した単語を下記から選び記入しなさい。本文の内容が
ヒントになるものもあります。

1. Her first really big success was in *Little Miss Sunshine*,
   a comedy about a family (   ) drive together across
   the United States.

   (A) they
   (B) which
   (C) who
   (D) where

2. No other actor ever nominated for an Academy Award
   was (   ) Abigail Breslin.

   (A) as younger as
   (B) young so as
   (C) as younger than
   (D) so young as

3. She says that if she stopped acting, she (   )
   become a veterinarian or fashion designer.

   (A) will
   (B) would
   (C) wants to
   (D) can

★5★ Nicolas Cage

Yumi : Do you believe in angels?
Ricky : That's a funny question. Why do you ask?
Yumi : Well, I was just reading about how people in many cultures and religions all have the idea of angels. Christians do. Muslims do. Buddhists do.
Ricky : I think we all just want to have the feeling that someone close is there to look after us. We all want a mother figure.
Yumi : That might be it. But it's funny how all these different cultures have the same idea, isn't it?
Ricky : I guess as human beings on the same planet, we are not all that different after all.

Nicolas Kim Coppola, was born in California in 1964. He grew up around many family members in entertainment. When he started to work in films, he changed his last name to Cage so that people wouldn't think he was getting jobs just because of his famous uncle, the film director Francis Ford Coppola. He got the name Cage from a comic book hero.

He has been in many films. Some of them have been very successful, and he won an Academy Award for his role in *Leaving Las Vegas* in 1996. At the same time, he has starred in a number of movies that were not successful either financially or with critics. Most of his successful movies are action movies.

Besides movies, he is very interested in comics. He started a comic series with his son, and another son is named after Superman's father. He is also interested in real estate. He has bought an island in the Bahamas, and two castles in Europe. Because of his real estate business, he has sometimes been in conflict with the American tax authorities, who have tried to take some of his houses in the United States away from him.

---

p24→ 1 **believe in**：〜の存在を信じる 2 **funny**：おかしい、面白い 4 **religion**：宗教 4 **angel**：天使 5 **Christian**:キリスト教徒 5 **Muslim**：イスラム教徒 5 **Buddhist**：仏教徒 p25→2 **entertainment**：芸能 3 **film**：映画、映画界 5 **film director**：映画監督 6 **Francis Ford Coppola**：フランシス・フォード・コッポラ、アメリカ合衆国の映画監督・映画プロデューサー・脚本家で多くの映画賞を受賞している 6 **comic book**：漫画雑誌 9 **Academy Award**：アカデミー賞・映画芸術科学アカデミー(AMPAS)が毎年最優秀映画及び映画関係者に与える賞。AMPAS：Academy of Motion Picture Arts and Sciences ・創立1927年で Hollywood にある映画芸術科学アカデミーのこと 13 **action movie**：アクション映画 16 **name after**：〜にちなんで名づける 16 **real estate**：不動産 17 **the Bahamas**：the Bahamas Islands ・フロリダ半島の南東に位置するバハマ諸島 19 **conflict**：闘争

THE LIVES AND TIMES OF MOVIE STARS

♥ Exercise 5-1 ♥
TF Quiz

以下の文章が本文の内容と合っていれば T 、誤りなら F を記入しなさい。

(　　) 1. Nicolas Cage was his original name.

(　　) 2. He has starred in a number of movies that were not successful either financially or with critics.

(　　) 3. Most of his successful movies are action movies.

(　　) 4. He suffered from being in conflict with the Internal Revenue Service.

(　　) 5. In addition to movies, he is interested in comics.

♥ Exercise 5-2 ♥
Japanese to English

以下の日本語の文章を英語に直しなさい。

両親が信じていた見解を信じるのは難しい。

_____

高い原油価格のせいで、彼は自動車を買うことを諦めた。

_____

Nicolas Cage

♥ Exercise 5-3 ♥
Structure and Vocabulary

次の空欄に文脈に即した単語を下記から選び記入しなさい。本文の内容が
ヒントになるものもあります。

1. Having interests in many fields, his life was (   )

   (A) fulfill
   (B) fully
   (C) full
   (D) fill

2. He has sometimes been (   ) with the American
   tax authorities.

   (A) in advance
   (B) in conflict
   (C) in focus
   (D) in haste

3. When he started to work in films, he changed his last
   name to Cage so that people wouldn't think he was
   getting jobs just (   ) his famous uncle, the film
   director Francis Ford Coppola.

   (A) despite
   (B) in spite of
   (C) in addition to
   (D) because of

★6★
Kevin Costner

Ricky :You know, my parents said there is something all Americans can tell you - where they were when they got the news that President Kennedy was shot.
Yumi :So where were you?
Ricky :Very funny. That was in 1963. A bit before my time. But my mother said she was at school. My father was sick at home sitting on the back balcony.
Yumi :Oh yeah?
Ricky :My father told me he was watching the motorcade on TV and he couldn't believe his eyes. Afterwards, the whole country just stopped. I guess something like that was a real shock in those days.

Kevin Costner

Kevin Michael Costner was born in 1955 in California. Because of his father's job, he had to move and go to many different schools when he was growing up. Later he said this made him have little confidence in himself.

He became interested in acting in his last year of university. After graduation he studied acting in the evenings. He first appeared in films in the early 1980s. By the end of the 1980s he started to play big roles in successful movies such as *Dances with Wolves*.

Besides acting, he is a country musician, singing in the group Kevin Costner & Modern West. He was playing in this group in 2009 in a concert when a stage collapsed and one person died. He is also interested in baseball and is the part-owner of a baseball team in Illinois.

He has seven children by three mothers. He lives on his ranch in Colorado. In Colorado he is active in politics and was a strong supporter to elect Barack Obama as president.

---

p28→ 3 **President Kennedy**：John F. Kennedy(1917-63)・米国の第35代大統領で Texas 州の Dallas で暗殺された 7 **back balcony:**裏のバルコニー 9 **motorcade**：重要人物を乗せた自動車行列のことで autocade ともいう 10 **afterwards:**後で 11 **guess**：推測する 12 **shock**：衝撃
p29→ 1 **California:**カリフォルニア・米国太平洋岸の州で州都 Sacramento 2 **because of:**〜のために 3 **grow up:**成長する 4 **make one have:**人に〜させる 4 **confidence**：自信 6 **university**：総合大学 6 **graduation**：卒業 7 **appear**：現れる 7 **in the early 1980s**：1890年代初期に **by the end of**：〜の終わりまでに 8 **big role**：大役 8 **successful**：成功した 10 **besides**：〜のほかに 10 **country musician**：カントリーミュージックの音楽家、演奏家 12 **concert**：コンサート 12 **collapse**：崩壊する 14 **part-owner:**共同所有者 14 **baseball team:**野球チーム 14 **Illinois:**イリノイ・米国中西部の州で州都は Springfield 16 **ranch**：牧場、放牧場 16 **Colorado**：コロラド・米国西部の州で州都は Denver 16 **politics**：政治運動 17 **elect**：選挙する 17 **president**：大統領

THE LIVES AND TIMES OF MOVIE STARS

♥ Exercise 6-1 ♥
TF Quiz

以下の文章が本文の内容と合っていれば T 、誤りなら F を記入しなさい。

(   ) 1. Kevin Michael Costner was born in the Southwest part of the US.

(   ) 2. He didn't go to university.

(   ) 3. By the end of the 1980s he started to play big roles in successful movies such as *Dances with Wolves*.

(   ) 4. One of his interests is baseball and he is the part-owner of a baseball team.

(   ) 5. He has three children by seven mothers.

♥ Exercise 6-2 ♥
Japanese to English

以下の日本語の文章を英語に直しなさい。

ここのところ、日本には多くの問題があるように思う。

_____

うちの犬は、4匹の雄との間に子犬を持った。

_____

Kevin Costner

♥ Exercise 6-3 ♥
Structure and Vocabulary

次の空欄に文脈に即した単語を下記から選び記入しなさい。本文の内容が
ヒントになるものもあります。

1. Because of his father's job, he (   ) move and go
   to many different schools when he was growing up.

   (A) has to

   (B) have to

   (C) must

   (D) had to

2. After (   ) from university he studied acting in
   the evenings.

   (A) undergraduate

   (B) graduating

   (C) graduation

   (D) grade

3. (   ) acting, he is a country musician, singing in
   the group Kevin Costner & Modern West.

   (A) In addition to

   (B) Due to

   (C) In contrast

   (D) In spite of

★7★
Russell Crowe

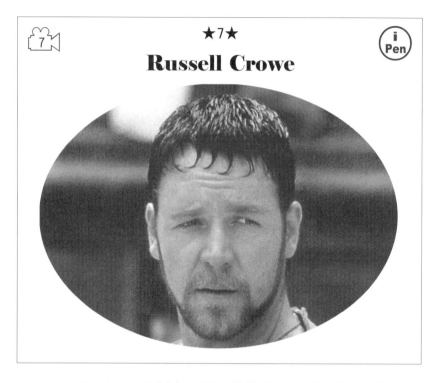

Ricky: I can't believe you like watching boxing. Two men fighting each other in public? If they did it on the street, the police would come.

Yumi: On the street nothing is controlled. In the ring there are rules and there is a referee. It's completely different.

Ricky: But it's still fighting. And you're the one who gets mad if two people even start speaking a bit loudly with each other.

Yumi: Again, that's without rules. You never know what the result will be if two people start arguing. Good friendships can be lost. Boxing is different. It's just entertainment.

Russell Ira Crowe was born in New Zealand in 1964. When he was very young, his family moved to Australia, where his parents worked preparing meals for film sets. With this connection, he had his first small television role when he was five or six years old. As a teenager, he moved with his family back to New Zealand.

He left high school at age sixteen to try to work as an actor. He moved back to Australia, where there were more opportunities for actors. His first big stage role was in *The Rocky Horror Show*. But because he could not always find work, he sometimes had to play music on the street to make money. His first big movies came in the 1990s. In the mid-1990s he started acting in the United States, where he has been nominated for an Oscar three times. He continues to make films today, but he has also become interested in promoting his rock group Russell Crowe & The Ordinary Fear of God.

He is now an Australian citizen. In 2009 the Australian Post Office put his picture on a postage stamp to mark his contributions as a world famous Australian actor.

---

p32→ ₂ **fighting**：けんか　₂ **in public**：面前で　₅ **referee**：審判員、レフェリー
₁₁ **result**：結果　₁₂ **friendship**：友情
p33→ ₁ **New　Zealand**：ニュージーランド・英連邦の国で首都 Wellington　₂ **Australia**
：オーストラリア連邦・正式名 Commonwealth of Australia で首都 Canberra
₉ **opportunity**：機会　₃ **prepare**：用意する、準備する　₃ **meal**：食事　₃ **film　set**：撮影用の映画のセット　₄ **connection**：つながり、交流　₈ **actor**：舞台・映画・テレビ俳優、特に男優　₁₄ **nominate**：候補に指名される　₁₄ **Oscar**：オスカー・米国映画芸術アカデミー賞受賞者に与えられる小型の黄金立像　₁₆ **promote**：宣伝販売する　₁₈ **citizen**
：市民　₁₈ **Australian　Post　Office**：オーストラリア郵政公社　₂₀ **contribution**：貢献

THE LIVES AND TIMES OF MOVIE STARS

♥ Exercise 7-1 ♥
TF Quiz

以下の文章が本文の内容と合っていれば T 、誤りなら F を記入しなさい。

(   )   1.   Russell Crowe was born in the 21st century in New Zealand.

(   )   2.   As a teenager, he moved with his family back to New Zealand.

(   )   3.   He left university to try to work as an actor.

(   )   4.   In 2009 the Australian Post Office put his picture on a postage stamp to mark his contributions as a world famous Australian actor.

(   )   5.   Now he has given up his movie career.

♥ Exercise 7-2 ♥
Japanese to English

以下の日本語の文章を英語に直しなさい。

ケーキを全部食べちゃったなんて、信じられない!

_____

新作の映画で、彼は小さな役をもらえることになっている。

_____

Russell Crowe

♥ Exercise 7-3 ♥
Structure and Vocabulary

次の空欄に文脈に即した単語を下記から選び記入しなさい。本文の内容が
ヒントになるものもあります。

1. On the street nothing is controlled. In the ring there are
    rules and there is a (   ).

    (A) reference

    (B) refereed

    (C) referee

    (D) refereeing

2. He sometimes had to play music on the street to make
    money. (   ) he could not always get work.

    (A) because

    (B) because of

    (C) but

    (D) for

3. He (   ) making films today, but he has also
    become interested in promoting his rock group Russell
    Crowe & The Ordinary Fear of God.

    (A) keeping

    (B) kept

    (C) keeps

    (D) keep

- 35 -

★8★
Michael J. Fox

Ricky :Who's that on TV, Yumi? I know him from somewhere.

Yumi :That's Michael J. Fox. Remember, from *Back to the Future*?

Ricky :Oh yeah. Where the teenage boy goes back in time thirty years, right?

Yumi :That's right. He meets his parents when they were still in high school. His mother is a teenager and she falls in love with him.

Ricky :Right. Pretty funny, that part! But you know, I don't think I would like to meet my parents as teenagers. Would you?

Yumi :I don't think my parents were ever teenagers.

Michael J. Fox was born Michael Andrew Fox in Alberta, Canada in 1961. He started acting on Canadian television when he was 15 years old. He never liked the name Andrew. But to register as an actor in the United States he couldn't use the same name as another actor, so he added "J."

With his new name he acted in many American television shows and movies. One of his most famous roles was in the three *Back to the Future* movies. Among his other films are *Bright Lights, Big City, Casualties of War,* and *The Frighteners.*

In 1990 he learned he had Parkinson's disease. This was very hard for him to accept, but in 1998 he told his fans about his disease. He started the Michael J. Fox Foundation to research ways of fighting Parkinson's disease. He supports politicians who are in favor of stem cell research against this disease. For this work he has received many awards.

---

p36→ ₂ **somewhere** ：どこかで ₃ **remember** ：思い出す ₇ **parent** ：親 ₈ **teenager** ：ティーンネイジャー ₉ **fall in love with** ：〜に恋する ₁₀ **pretty** ：本当に、かなり ₁₁ **I would like to** ：〜したい

p37→₂ **Alberta** ：アルバータ・カナダ西部の州 ₂ **Canada** ：カナダ・北米大陸北部の国で首都は Ottawa ₄ **register** ：登録する ₅ **the same name** 〜 **as** …：……と同じ〜 ₆ **add** ：加える ₈ **role** ：役割 ₉ **among** ：〜の間 ₁₂ **learn** ：学ぶ ₁₂ **Parkinson's disease:** パーキンソン病・ J.パーキンソンの報告した疾患で、筋肉の緊張が高まり、随意運動を開始することが困難になるなどの症状で高齢者に多く発する ₁₃ **hard** ：困難な ₁₃ **accept** ：受け入れる ₁₃ **fan** ：ファン ₁₄ **foundation** ：財団 ₁₅ **research** ：研究する ₁₅ **fight** ：戦う ₁₆ **politician** ：政治家 ₁₆ **in favor of** ：〜を好んで ₁₆ **stem cell** ：幹細胞・血球のように特殊な細胞を生み出す未分化の細胞 ₁₈ **receive** ：受け取る ₁₈ **award** ：賞

THE LIVES AND TIMES OF MOVIE STARS

♥ Exercise 8-1 ♥
TF Quiz

以下の文章が本文の内容と合っていれば T、誤りなら F を記入しなさい。

（　）1. Michael J. Fox was born in Alberta, Canada in the 20th century.

（　）2. He started his acting career on American television with the name Andrew.

（　）3. *Back to the Future* is known as one of the most famous movies he performed in.

（　）4. In 1990 he peacefully accepted the fact that he had Parkinson's disease.

（　）5. His foundation, the Michael J. Fox Foundation, was created to help advance promising research path to cure Parkinson's disease, including embryonic stem cell studies.

♥ Exercise 8-2 ♥
Japanese to English

以下の日本語の文章を英語に直しなさい。

スーザンを高校生のころから知っている。

私は愛知県で教員として登録されている。

Michael J. Fox

♥ Exercise 8-3 ♥
Structure and Vocabulary

次の空欄に文脈に即した単語を下記から選び記入しなさい。本文の内容が
ヒントになるものもあります。

1. He starred in the Canadian television series *Leo and Me* at the age of fifteen, and three years later, moved to Los Angeles to (   ) an acting career.

    (A) pursuing

    (B) pursue

    (C) pursued

    (D) pursuer

2. Symptoms of Parkinson's disease may be mild at first. (   ), you may have a mild tremor or a slight feeling that one leg or foot is stiff and dragging.

    (A) For appearance's sake

    (B) For the taking

    (C) For this time

    (D) For instance

3. He supports politicians who are in favor of stem cell (   ) against this disease.

    (A) study

    (B) workshop

    (C) deal

    (D) information

★9★
Mark Hamil

Yumi :I had such an interesting day today.
Ricky :Oh yeah? What did you do?
Yumi :I was home visiting my parents and spent the afternoon going through some of the things they have of mine still.
Ricky :Oh, that's always interesting. Did you find some old love letters from all the boys in school?
Yumi :Nothing like that. I'm talking about old comic books. I have a whole box of them. I spent all afternoon reading them. I felt like a little girl again.
Ricky :Sounds like fun. And a bit safer than finding old love letters maybe!

Mark Richard Hamil was born in California in 1951. Because his father was in the U.S. Navy, he grew up living in several places, including Yokosuka near Tokyo. After graduating from high school, he studied drama at Los Angeles City College. His first acting work was in television shows and cartoons.

He got his most famous role as Luke Skywalker in the *Star Wars* series when a friend tried to get the part and failed. The friend suggested that Hamil try out for the part, and Hamil was lucky. During the actual filming he was not so lucky, however. Just before finishing filming, he was in a very bad car accident that broke bones in several parts of his face.

After *Star Wars*, he was in a number of stage plays, which were very successful. He was also in a number of different kinds of movies and television shows. Many of these had something to do with *Star Wars*. He has also been a voice actor. As a voice actor he is especially famous for playing evil villains in cartoons, anime, and video games. He has always liked comic books and has even written a comic book series himself.

---

p40→ 1 **interesting**：おもしろい　6 **love letter**：ラブレター　8 **comic book**：漫画本
p41→ 2 **navy**：海軍　4 **Los Angeles City College**：ロサンゼルス・シティ・カレッジ・カリフォルニア州ロサンゼルスのノースバーモントアヴェニューにある公立の短期大学
6 **cartoon**：アニメ　9 **suggest**：提案する　9 **try out**：適性試験を受ける、オーディションを受ける　12 **car accident**：自動車の事故　12 **break**：折る　12 **bone**：骨
14 **stage play**：舞台劇　17 **have something to do with**：〜と何か関係がある
18 **voice actor**：男性の声優　19 **evil**：邪悪な　19 **villain**：劇や小説や映画などの悪役
19 **anime**：アニメ　19 **video game**：テレビゲーム　21 **comic book**：漫画雑誌

THE LIVES AND TIMES OF MOVIE STARS

♥ Exercise 9-1 ♥
TF Quiz

以下の文章が本文の内容と合っていれば T、誤りなら F を記入しなさい。

(   ) 1. Because his father was in the U.S. Navy, he grew up living in several places such as Okinawa.

(   ) 2. After graduating from high school, he studied journalism at Los Angeles City College.

(   ) 3. He got his most famous role as Luke Skywalker in the *Star Wars* series

(   ) 4. After *Star Wars*, he was in a number of stage plays, which were very successful.

(   ) 5. He has always liked comic books and has even written a comic book series himself.

♥ Exercise 9-2 ♥
Japanese to English

以下の日本語の文章を英語に直しなさい。

えっ、本当？　きみのことが全く信じられない！

_____

英語の教師として、私は時々校長に代わって翻訳をしなければ
ならない。

_____

Mark Hamil

♥ Exercise 9-3 ♥
Structure and Vocabulary

次の空欄に文脈に即した単語を下記から選び記入しなさい。本文の内容が
ヒントになるものもあります。

1. His first acting (   ) was in television shows and
    cartoons.

    (A) cast
    (B) life
    (C) part-time
    (D) work

2. (   ) the actual filming he was not so lucky,
    however.

    (A) According to
    (B) Due to
    (C) When
    (D) During

3. As a voice actor he is especially famous for playing
    (   ) villains in cartoons, anime, and video
    games.

    (A) simple
    (B) pure
    (C) evil
    (D) corrective

THE LIVES AND TIMES OF MOVIE STARS

★10★
Tom Hanks

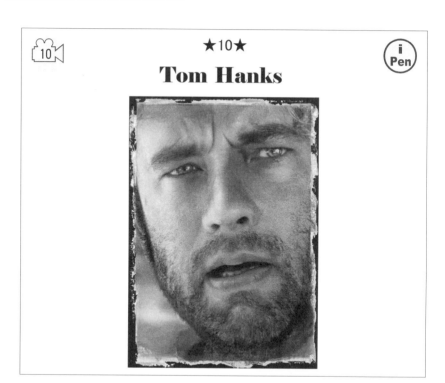

Ricky :Wow, what a great movie that was!
Yumi :Yeah, it makes you think if you could survive on an island all by yourself if you were cast away like Tom Hanks was.
5 Ricky :And left with only a ball for a friend.
Yumi :I think I could fish and get fruit, but just think how hard it would be to get food to fill your stomach, like rice or potatoes.
Ricky :And what if you cut yourself and got an infection?
10 Yumi :That's true. And I guess the biggest problem would be getting fresh water. An island in the sun sounds great, but you wouldn't survive long without any rain.

Tom Hanks

Thomas Jeffrey Hanks was born in 1956 in California. He is a distant relative of President Lincoln. His parents divorced when he was young, and grew up with his father. He and his brother and sister often had to look after themselves when their father was working. This made them very independent.

He studied acting at university and was very interested in the theater. He became an intern at a theater and did not finish university.

After a bit of stage acting, he acted for TV and then movies. Some of his early movies were successful, but some were not. He won his first Academy Award in 1993 for his role in *Philadelphia* and his second the next year for his role in *Forrest Gump*. Besides acting, he has also produced movies and has his own record and film production company. He has earned more money at the box office than any other actor.

He is a very active supporter of both environmental and gay rights issues. He also supports space exploration. Asteroid 12818 Tomhanks was named after him.

---

p44→ ₂ survive：生き抜く　₃ by yourself：独りぼっちで　₃ cast away：漂流させる　₇ fill your stomach：お腹いっぱいになる　₈ potato：ジャガイモ　₉ infection：感染症　₁₀ That's true.：その通り　₁₀ the biggest problem：最大の問題　₁₁ fresh water：新鮮な水、真水　₁₂ survive：生き残る　₁₂ without：～なしで

p45→₂ distant relative:遠い親戚 ₂ President Lincoln:Abraham Lincoln(1809-65)・米国の第16代大統領 ₃ divorce：離婚する　₃ grow up：成長する　₈ theater：劇場　₈ intern：研修生　₁₅ produce：制作する　₁₅ film production company：映画製作会社　₁₆ earn：稼ぐ　₁₆ box office：興業の売り上げ　₁₈ environmental:環境の　₁₉ gay rights：同性愛者の権利　₁₉ issue：問題　₁₉ exploration：探索　₂₀ asteroid：小惑星

THE LIVES AND TIMES OF MOVIE STARS

♥ Exercise 10-1 ♥
TF Quiz

以下の文章が本文の内容と合っていれば T 、誤りなら F を記入しなさい。

( ) 1. Thomas Jeffrey Hanks was born in 1956 in California. He is a grandchild of President Lincoln.

( ) 2. He graduated from university with top honors.

( ) 3. Some of his early movies were successful, but however, some were not.

( ) 4. His second Academy Award was in 1993.

( ) 5. The only cause he supports is exploration of the solar system.

♥ Exercise 10-2 ♥
Japanese to English

以下の日本語の文章を英語に直しなさい。

このような本が、人生について真剣に考えさせたんですね。

_____

この通りは、月を最初に歩いた人物にちなんで、アームストロング通りと名付けられた。

_____

- 46 -

Tom Hanks

♥ Exercise 10-3 ♥
Structure and Vocabulary

次の空欄に文脈に即した単語を下記から選び記入しなさい。本文の内容が
ヒントになるものもあります。

1. I think I could fish and get fruit, but just think how hard
    it would be to get food to (   ) your stomach,
    like rice or potatoes.

    (A) filling
    (B) fully
    (C) full
    (D) fill

2. He got an internship at a theater. (   ) he left
    the university.

    (A) Due to
    (B) Because of
    (C) That's why
    (D) Why

3. Forrest Gump was not an intelligent guy, and was
    (   ) at many historic moments by accident, but
    his true love, Jenny Curran, eluded him.

    (A) proved
    (B) present
    (C) proposed
    (D) purpose

- 47 -

★11★
Anne Hathaway

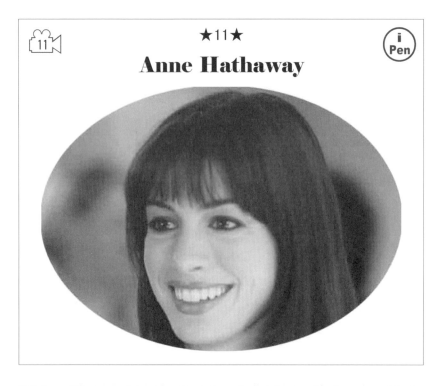

Ricky :Those girls we had lunch with - all they could do was talk about fashion.
Yumi :I know. Their lives circle around getting the latest Gucci bag or worrying that they don't have this year's spring colors. Fashion is meant to be fun, not a life.
Ricky :Well, it's a life to the people who are taking the girls' money.
Yumi :You can say that again. The devil certainly does wear Prada.
Ricky :And the devil isn't cheap either, is he?
Yumi :I'd prefer to be an angel in hand-me-downs.

Anne Hathaway

Anne Jacqueline Hathaway was born in New York City in 1982. Her mother was an actress and encouraged her to be an actress also. Anne herself wanted to be a nun when she was young, but after she learned that her brother was gay, she left the Catholic church because of its anti-gay teachings. She was in many school plays as a student, and had a full-time part in a television show when she was sixteen years old.

In the early part of this century, she had many successful film roles. Many of these were family-oriented films, and she is often thought of especially as a children's movie star. In recent years she has appeared in more films made for adult audiences. These included *Brokeback Mountain*, a gay romance, and *The Devil Wears Prada*, about the fashion industry. For the latter film she had to lose a lot of weight. To do this she went on a very strict diet of fish, fruit, and vegetables. She continues to make a number of movies each year and she is active in supporting several charities.

---

p48→ ₃ **circle around**：取り囲む　₄ **Gucci**：グッチ・イタリアの高級ブランド　₉ **devil**：悪魔　₁₀ **Prada**：プラダ・イタリアの高級ブランド　₁₂ **prefer**：好む　₁₂ **angel**：天使　₁₂ **hand-me-downs**：お下がり

p49→ ₁ **New York City**：ニューヨークシティ・New York 州南東端の Hudson 河口にある都市　₂ **encourage**：励ます　₃ **actress**：女優　₃ **nun**：修道女　₅ **Catholic church**：カトリック教会　₅ **because of**：〜のために　₅ **anti-gay**：反同性愛者　₇ **full-time**：フルタイムの　₉ **century**：世紀　₁₀ **film role**：映画の役割　₁₀ **family-oriented**：家族中心の　₁₂ **in recent years**：近年では　₁₃ **audience**：聴衆、観衆　₁₃ **include**：含む　₁₄ **fashion industry**：ファッション業界　₁₅ **lose a lot of weight**：体重を多く減らす　₁₆ **diet**：食事療法　₁₇ **vegetable**：野菜　₁₇ **continue**：続ける　₁₇ **a number of**：多数の　₁₈ **charity**：慈善

THE LIVES AND TIMES OF MOVIE STARS

♥ Exercise 11-1 ♥
TF Quiz

以下の文章が本文の内容と合っていれば T 、誤りなら F を記入しなさい。

(   )   1.   Anne Hathaway was born in New York City. Her mother was an actress and encouraged her to be an actress also.

(   )   2.   She left the Catholic church because of its anti-homosexuality teachings.

(   )   3.   Many of her films were family-oriented films, and she is often thought of especially as an adults' movie star in the early part of this century.

(   )   4.   *Brokeback Mountain*, in which she played a main role, was gay romance.

(   )   5.   She continues to make a number of movies each year and she is active in supporting several charities.

♥ Exercise 11-2 ♥
Japanese to English

以下の日本語の文章を英語に直しなさい。

彼女がしたことは、新聞を読んだことだった。

_____

彼は紛れもなく戦争反対を唱える政治家だ。

_____

- 50 -

Anne Hathaway

♥ Exercise 11-3 ♥
Structure and Vocabulary

次の空欄に文脈に即した単語を下記から選び記入しなさい。本文の内容が
ヒントになるものもあります。

1. She was in many school plays as a student, (   )
   had a full-time part in a television show when she was
   sixteen years old.

   (A) but
   (B) and
   (C) for
   (D) with

2. In recent years she has (   ) in more films made
   for adult audiences.

   (A) appearing
   (B) appear
   (C) appeared
   (D) appearance

3. For the latter film she had to lose (   ) weight.
   To do this she went on a very strict diet of fish, fruit,
   and vegetables.

   (A) most
   (B) every
   (C) a lot of
   (D) many

★12★
Audrey Hepburn

Ricky :Welcome back. How was the holiday? Have a good time?
Yumi :More like a Roman Holiday.
Ricky :Huh? What do you mean?
Yumi :You've never heard the phrase? A "Roman Holiday" means something that is supposed to be entertaining, but it is really full of violence and suffering.
Ricky :Oh, I see. Like the old Roman gladiators fighting in public. So, uh, I guess the holiday wasn't so great?
Yumi :Not at all. I went with the people from work, and they were always fighting and arguing. I didn't enjoy it at all.

Audrey Hepburn

Audrey Kathleen Ruston was born in Belgium in 1929. She was later famous under the name **Audrey Hepburn**. Her father had a British father and an Austrian mother, while her mother was Dutch. She grew up speaking five languages. She went to school in the Netherlands during the German occupation, hiding under a Dutch surname. She had studied ballet, and during the war danced in secret performances to raise money for the Dutch resistance against the Germans. Because of her suffering and hunger during the war, she worked later in life to support UNICEF.

After the war she continued as a ballerina. She appeared in a Dutch movie in 1948. After this she moved to London to study ballet. To make a living, she started acting, which ended up being her main work instead of ballet. She worked both on stage and in British movies. She got her first big role in *Roman Holiday*.

After this big success, she made many other movies. She was well known for being "elfish" and very chic. Some of her movies were the most successful in the twentieth century. Her last work was a television series that went to air one day after she died in 1993.

---

p52→ 1 **holiday**：休日、祭日 1 **have a good time**：楽しい時を過ごす 5 **phrase**：フレーズ、言い回し 6 **be supposed to:**～することになっている 7 **entertain:**楽しませる 7 **be full of:**～で一杯である 7 **violence:**暴力 8 **suffering:**苦痛 9 **I see.:**なるほど in public：公共の場で 9 **gladiator**：古代ローマの剣闘士 12 **argue**：議論する
p53→ 1 **Belgium**：ベルギー・ヨーロッパ西部北海沿岸の王国で、首都は Brussels 4 **Dutch**：オランダの 6 **surname**：名字、姓 5 **the Netherlands**：オランダ・Holland の公式名 6 **occupation**：職業 7 **ballet**：バレエ 8 **raise**：（金を）集める 8 **resistance**：抵抗 9 **hunger**：飢餓 11 **ballerina**：バレリーナ 13 **make a living**：生計を立てる 13 **acting**：演技 18 **elfish**：小妖精のような 18 **chic**：粋な、あかぬけした 19 **the twentieth century**：20世紀 20 **air**：放送

THE LIVES AND TIMES OF MOVIE STARS

♥ Exercise 12-1 ♥
TF Quiz

以下の文章が本文の内容と合っていれば T 、誤りなら F を記入しなさい。

(　　) 1. Audrey Hepburn was born in Belgium in the first half of the 20th century.

(　　) 2. Audrey Hepburn had a British father and an Austrian mother.

(　　) 3. During the German occupation, Audrey Hepburn worked for UNICEF.

(　　) 4. Audrey Hepburn moved to London in order to become an actress because she realized that she was not good at ballet any more.

(　　) 5. Audrey Hepburn passed away in 1993, which was when her last work went to air.

♥ Exercise 12-2 ♥
Japanese to English

以下の日本語の文章を英語に直しなさい。

私は決してその言葉を忘れないだろう。

_____

高校を卒業しないで生計を立てていくのは難しい。

_____

- 54 -

Audrey Hepburn

♥ Exercise 12-3 ♥
Structure and Vocabulary

次の空欄に文脈に即した単語を下記から選び記入しなさい。本文の内容が
ヒントになるものもあります。

1. She had studied ballet, and during the war danced in secret performances to (   ) money for the Dutch resistance against the Germans.

    (A) pay

    (B) save

    (C) send

    (D) raise

2. After this, acting (   ) being her main work instead of ballet.

    (A) keep up

    (B) ended up

    (C) keep on

    (D) carry on

3. Some of her movies were the most (   ) in the twentieth century.

    (A) succeed

    (B) success

    (C) successful

    (D) succeeded

★13★
Harrison Ford

Yumi :That was such a good movie. It makes you think what would happen if you were sent to jail for something you didn't do.
Ricky :I know. And it does happen from time to time, doesn't it?
Yumi :It does indeed. So, Ricky, would you run away and hide or would you just go with the police?
Ricky :That's a tough question. I'd like to think the courts would find out the truth, but it doesn't always happen like that.
Yumi :I know. Let's hope we never have to worry about that, eh?

Harrison Ford was born in Chicago in 1942. Both his parents had once been actors. Growing up, he was a very active Boy Scout and he became a Life Scout, a very high level. He was also a radio announcer as a student. At university he took a drama class because he thought he was too shy. He moved to California after university and got small parts in movies. His first bigger roles were in television shows. He also worked as a stagehand.

In the 1970s he got his first important movie roles. After that he got bigger and bigger roles, including *Star Wars*, *The Fugitive*, and *Raiders of the Lost Ark*. Recently he has often appeared in several famous commercials on Japanese television.

He has his own ranch in Wyoming. He relaxes as a private airplane and helicopter pilot both in Wyoming and California. He is a very strong supporter of nature conservation. Both a species of spiders and a species of ants have been named after him. He is also a supporter of Tibetan independence and against the American war in Iraq.

---

p56→　2 **jail**：刑務所　　4 **from time to time**：しばしば、時々　　6 **indeed**：本当に
7 **hide**：隠れる　　8 **court**：法廷　　12 **eh**：えっ、ひゃー・話し手の驚きや疑いを示す
p57→　1 **Chicago**：シカゴ・ Illinois 州 Michigan 湖畔にある米国第3の都市　　3 **Boy Scout**：ボーイ・スカウト　　3 **Life Scout**：ボーイスカウトは11～17歳までで、米国では tenderfoot(初級)、second class(2級)、first class(1級)、star scout 、life scout 、eagle scout と進級する。4 **radio announcer:**ラジオのアナウンサー　　8 **stagehand:**舞台係　　14 **ranch**：牧場、放牧場　　14 **Wyoming**：ワイオミング・米国北西部の州で、州都は Cheyenne　　15 **airplane**：飛行機　　15 **helicopter**：ヘリコプター　　17 **conservation**：保護　　17 **a species of**：一種の　　17 **spider**：蜘蛛　　19 **Iraq**：イラク・アジア南西部の共和国で首都は Baghdad　　19 **Tibetan**：チベットの　　19 **Independence**：独立

THE LIVES AND TIMES OF MOVIE STARS

♥ Exercise 13-1 ♥
TF Quiz

以下の文章が本文の内容と合っていれば T 、誤りなら F を記入しなさい。

( ) 1. Harrison Ford was born in Chicago in 1942. Both his parents had once been actors.

( ) 2. At university he took a drama class because he thought he was too shy.

( ) 3. Recently he has often appeared in several famous Japanese movies.

( ) 4. He has his own ranch in Wyoming.

( ) 5. Both a species of spiders and a species of ants have been named after him.

♥ Exercise 13-2 ♥
Japanese to English

以下の日本語の文章を英語に直しなさい。

私は時々仕事で東京へ行く。

_____

彼女はとても活動的な組合員だ。

_____

- 58 -

Harrison Ford

♥ Exercise 13-3 ♥
Structure and Vocabulary

次の空欄に文脈に即した単語を下記から選び記入しなさい。本文の内容が
ヒントになるものもあります。

1. (   ), he was a very active Boy Scout and he
   became a Life Scout, a very high level.

   (A) Grow up
   (B) Growing up
   (C) Grew up
   (D) Grown

2. That's a (   )question. I'd like to think the courts
   would find out the truth, but it doesn't always happen
   like that.

   (A) hazardous
   (B) hard
   (C) humid
   (D) heard

3. He is also a supporter of Tibetan (   ) and
   against the American war in Iraq.

   (A) independent
   (B) independently
   (C) independence
   (D) dependence

THE LIVES AND TIMES OF MOVIE STARS

★14★
Whitney Houston

Yumi :I wonder what it would be like to be a bodyguard.
Ricky :You mean of a famous person?
Yumi :Yeah. You would always be there and so you would get to know everything about the person, the good things and the bad things, all the private stuff. But it would be business, not like a friend.
Ricky :I think you would have to become a friend. If not, you would hate your job. You couldn't be together with someone so much and not like them. You would become crazy and hate your job.
Yumi :But I think if you became too close, you would feel awkward taking money from him or her.

Whitney Houston

Whitney Elizabeth Houston was born in New Jersey, USA in 1963. Her mother was a gospel singer and other people in her family were also very famous singers. She started singing at church when she was a child. When she was a teenager, she would sometimes travel with her mother and sing on stage with her. She became a backup recording singer when she was a teenager.

For a while as a teenager she was a fashion model. At the same time she worked as a singer. Several companies wanted her to sign recording contracts, but her mother said she must finish high school first. After high school she released her first album. She became an international soul and R&B star in the 1980s. She also became active in projects to help poor youth, especially youth with HIV.

She made her first movie, *The Bodyguard*, in 1992. She made several other movies before she died. In her last years she had problems with drugs, especially cocaine. She drowned in a bathtub in 2012.

---

p60→ ₁ **wonder**：不思議に思う ₁ **bodyguard**：警護 ₂ **famous**：有名な ₅ **private**：個人的な ₈ **hate**：嫌う ₈ **together**：一緒に ₁₂ **awkward**：不器用な、ぎこちない
p61→ ₁ **New Jersey**：ニュージャージー・米国東部の州で州都は Trenton ₂ **gospel singer**：ゴスペル調の歌手 ₅ **teenager**：ティーンエイジャー、10代の少年・少女 ₆ **on stage**：舞台で ₆ **backup recording singer**：バックアップの録音歌手 ₈ **for a while**：しばらくの間 ₈ **fashion model**：ファッションモデル ₉ **at the same time**：同時に ₁₀ **sign**：(契約を) 結ぶ ₁₀ **contract**：契約 ₁₂ **soul**：soul music ・ブルース・ゴスペル等の混合した黒人音楽 ₁₃ **R & B**：rhythm and blues ・ブルースのリズムを強調した黒人霊歌の特徴を持つ黒人音楽 ₁₄ **HIV**：human immunodeficiency virus ・ヒト免疫不全ウイルス、エイズウイルス ₁₇ **drug**：ドラッグ、麻薬 ₁₇ **cocaine**：コカイン ₁₈ **drown**：溺れ死ぬ ₁₈ **bathtub**：浴槽

THE LIVES AND TIMES OF MOVIE STARS

♥ Exercise 14-1 ♥
TF Quiz

以下の文章が本文の内容と合っていれば T 、誤りなら F を記入しなさい。

(　　)　1. Whitney Houston was born in New Jersey, USA in 1963. Her mother was a gospel singer and other people in her family were also very famous singers.

(　　)　2. She would sometimes travel with her mother and sing on stage with her when she was twenty years old.

(　　)　3. She worked as a singer when she was a teenager.

(　　)　4. Her first album was released after graduating from high school.

(　　)　5. In her last years she had problems with drugs, especially cocaine.

♥ Exercise 14-2 ♥
Japanese to English

以下の日本語の文章を英語に直しなさい。

ビル・ゲイツのようなお金持ちになるのって、どんな感じだろう。

_____

しばらくの間、私は修道女になりたかった。

_____

- 62 -

Whitney Houston

♥ Exercise 14-3 ♥
Structure and Vocabulary

次の空欄に文脈に即した単語を下記から選び記入しなさい。本文の内容が
ヒントになるものもあります。

1. She also became active in projects to help poor youth,
   (   ) youth with HIV.

   (A) especially

   (B) except

   (C) exclude

   (D) expected

2. Several companies wanted her to (   ) recording
   contracts, but her mother said she must finish high
   school first.

   (A) fix

   (B) register

   (C) make

   (D) take

3. Because of problems with drugs, she struggled and
   drowned (   ).

   (A) end

   (B) final

   (C) in the end

   (D) result

- 63 -

★15★
Samuel L. Jackson

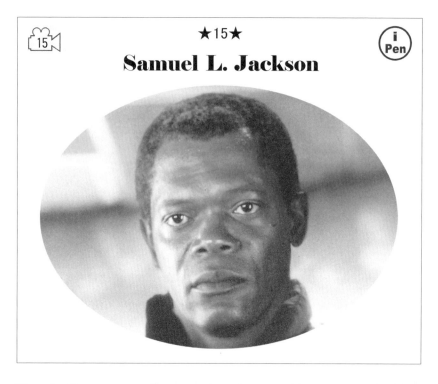

Yumi :If you were in a movie, do you think you would like to see yourself?
Ricky :You mean watch the movie? No way! I hate even listening to myself on a tape recording. Why do you ask?
Yumi :I was just reading that Samuel Jackson always watches his own movies. He goes to a regular theater, buys a ticket, and watches the movie with everybody else.
Ricky :Wow, imagine you're at the movies, the movie finishes and the lights go on, and there's the actor sitting right next to you! I bet some people really get a shock!

Samuel L. Jackson

Samuel Leroy Jackson was born in Washington, D.C. in 1948, but he grew up in Tennessee. Although he planned on studying marine biology, when he went to Morehouse College after high school, he joined an acting group and decided to study drama.

After Martin Luther King was killed, he became active in civil rights protests. Together with other students, he held university officials hostage so that university policies would change. He was a strong supporter of Black Power and the use of force to fight against American racism.

He started acting in films in 1972. He has been a very successful actor, starring in more than one hundred movies.

One of these was *The Negotiator*, where he played a a policeman who takes hostages to break a corrupt group of police officers. According to *The Guinness World Records*, in 2011 he became the highest earning actor of all time.

Although he was successful in his work, he had problems with very serious drug addiction. He was able to stop his addiction only after a long stay in a special clinic in the 1990s.

---

p64→ ₈ **theater**：劇場、映画館　₈ **ticket**：チケット　₁₀ **imagine**：想像する　₁₂ **bet**：きっと～とだと断言する、予期する
p65→ ₁ **Washington, D.C.**：ワシントン・米国の首都で D.C.は District of Columbia の略 ₂ **grow up**：成長する　₂ **Tennessee**：テネシー：米国南東部の州で、州都は Nashville ₃ **plan**：計画する　₃ **marine biology**:海洋生物学　₅ **drama**:演劇 ₆ **Martin Luther King**：キング牧師・アフリカ系アメリカ公民権運動の指導者である　₇ **civil rights**：市民権　₇ **protest**：抗議　₈ **university officials**：大学職員　₈ **hostage**：人質　₈ **policy**：政策　₉ **Black Power**：ブラックパワー・自分たちの権力機構を設立しようという米国黒人運動のスローガン　₁₀ **force**：勢力　₁₀ **fight**：戦う　₁₀ **racism**：人種差別　₁₁ **star**：主演する　₁₄ **policeman**：警察官　₁₄ **corrupt**：不正な　₁₈ **drug addiction**：薬物依存　₁₉ **clinic**：診療所、医院

THE LIVES AND TIMES OF MOVIE STARS

♥ Exercise 15-1 ♥
TF Quiz

以下の文章が本文の内容と合っていれば T、誤りなら F を記入しなさい。

(   ) 1. Born in Washington, Samuel Leroy Jackson grew up in Tennessee.

(   ) 2. He was originally going to study marine biology, but he became interested in drama while he was at College.

(   ) 3. He fought against racism in the United States when Martin Luther King was still alive.

(   ) 4. According to *The Guinness World Records*, he became the highest earning actor of 2011.

(   ) 5. He was seriously addicted to drugs but not any more.

♥ Exercise 15-2 ♥
Japanese to English

以下の日本語の文章を英語に直しなさい。

私はいい加減に仕事をするのが嫌いだ。

_____

6年間英語を勉強してきたけれど、彼は英語を上手に話せない。

_____

Samuel L. Jackson

♥ Exercise 15-3 ♥
Structure and Vocabulary

次の空欄に文脈に即した単語を下記から選び記入しなさい。本文の内容が
ヒントになるものもあります。

1. After Martin Luther King was killed, he became
   (   ) in civil rights protests.

   (A) passive
   (B) active
   (C) strong
   (D) weak

2. According to *The Guinness World Records*, in 2011 he
   became the (   ) earning actor of all time.

   (A) most
   (B) best
   (C) highest
   (D) much

3. He was (   ) to stop his addiction only after a long
   stay in a special clinic in the 1990s.

   (A) able
   (B) unable
   (C) recovered
   (D) overcome

★16★
Nicole Kidman

Ricky :At work today we all collected money to give to UNICEF.

Yumi :Really? We did, too, last week. One of the women at work was reading an article about Nicole Kidman and was telling us about it. We all said if she can do something for poor children, we can too.

Ricky :I think that must have been the same article that got our office doing the same thing. One of the secretaries told our boss about the article she was reading and the two of them organized a fund-raising. Our boss said he would give two dollars for every dollar we collected.

Nicole Mary Kidman was born in 1967 in Honolulu. Because her parents are Australian and she was born in the United States, she is both an Australian and an American citizen. Her family returned to Australia before she started school, and she grew up in Sydney. When she was young she was very shy and even had a stutter. After high school she studied drama in Melbourne and Sydney, but actually had her first film role when she was sixteen.

By the time she was twenty, she had been in several films and television shows. Since then she has been in many successful American, Australian and British films. She has also recorded some songs. One of them was number one on the UK charts.

She is an active worker for charities. She was a "Goodwill Ambassador" for UNICEF in 1994 and a "Goodwill Ambassador" for the United Nations Development Fund for Women in 2006. In 2004, the United Nations named her a "Citizen of the World." She was made a Companion of the Order of Australia in 2006. This is the highest award from the Australian government.

---

p68→ ₁**collect**：集める ₂**UNICEF**： United Nations International Children's Emergency・国連児童基金、ユニセフ（現在は United Nations Children's Fund であるが略称は同じである） ₄**article**：記事 ₉**secretary**：秘書 ₉**boss**：上司 ₁₀**organize**：組織する ₁₀**fund-raising**：基金募集、カンパ活動

p69→ ₁**Honolulu**：ホノルル・米国 Hawaii 州の州都で Oahu 島の港市 ₂**Australia**： Commonwealth of Australia・オーストラリア連邦で首都は Canberra ₅**Sydney**：シドニー・オーストラリア南東部の海港 ₆**stutter**：どもること ₇**Melbourne**：メルボルン・オーストラリア南東部の港市 ₈**actually**：実際に ₉**by the time**：〜までに ₁₃**UK**： the United Kingdom of Great Britain and Northern Ireland・連合王国、英国で首都は London ₁₅**Goodwill Ambassador**：親善大使 ₁₇**United Nations**：国際連合・本部は New York 市 ₁₈**citizen of the world**：世界市民 ₂₀**government**：政府

THE LIVES AND TIMES OF MOVIE STARS

♥ Exercise 16-1 ♥
TF Quiz

以下の文章が本文の内容と合っていれば T 、誤りなら F を記入しなさい。

(   ) 1. Her citizenship is both Australian and American.

(   ) 2. Her family moved to Australia before she started school, and she grew up in Melbourne.

(   ) 3. She has also released some songs. One of them was number one on the US charts.

(   ) 4. She was a "Goodwill Ambassador" for UNICEF in 2006.

(   ) 5. The companion of the Order of Australia, which she received in 2006, is the highest award from the Australian government.

♥ Exercise 16-2 ♥
Japanese to English

以下の日本語の文章を英語に直しなさい。

えっ、去年のクリスマスにあなたもオーストラリアに行っていたって、本当?

_____

40歳になるまでに、私は大きな会社の社長になりたい。

_____

Nicole Kidman

♥ Exercise 16-3 ♥
Structure and Vocabulary

次の空欄に文脈に即した単語を下記から選び記入しなさい。本文の内容が
ヒントになるものもあります。

1. One of the women at work was reading an article
   (   ) Nicole Kidman and was telling us about it.

   (A) with

   (B) about

   (C) out

   (D) for

2. It's hard to move to a foreign country as an (   ),
   because the culture is completely different.

   (A) immoralist

   (B) irony

   (C) innocent

   (D) immigrant

3. UNICEF (   ) the United Nations Children's
   Fund.

   (A) meaning

   (B) express

   (C) appear

   (D) stands for

★17★
Youki Kudoh

Yumi :I just finished watching *Snow Falling on Cedar*. I didn't know there was so much feeling against Japanese Americans even after the war.

Ricky :In a way it is understandable, after the attack on Pearl Harbor by the Japanese and everything that happened in World War II. But I feel sorry for the Nikkeis. My grandmother is Nikkei, you know. Even though her parents were born in the United States, they were put into camps just as if they were foreigners from Japan.

Yumi :She must have felt really angry.

Ricky :All her life. I'm glad she lived long enough to get an apology from the US government in 1990.

Youki Kudoh was born in Tokyo in 1971. Her father was a famous *enka* singer, Hachiro Isawa. She said later that having such a famous father made it difficult sometimes to prove that her success was due to her own talent, not to her father's name. She began her public career as a singer when she was twelve years old. She had her first big role in a movie when she was still a young teenager. This was for the movie *The Crazy Family*. She won an award for the best new actor for this role at the Yokohama Film Festival.

She is fluent in French and English. Besides her success as a singer and as an actress in Japanese films and television shows, she has starred in overseas films. Her first big hit was in an Australian thriller in 1997. As a result, she is often a public face of Japan to other countries.

She once said in an interview that Japanese need to have more confidence in their own cultural values. She said that the strong influence of American values and culture in Japan was really the fault of Japanese people themselves.

She likes to be in nature and is a passionate diver. Several years ago, she moved for a time to the countryside to spend time farming.

---

p72→ ₃**Japanese   Americans**：日系アメリカ人　₄**understandable**：理解できる、予想された ₄**attack**：攻撃　₅**Pearl Harbor**：真珠湾・米国 Hawaii 州の軍港で1941年12月8日（日本時間）に日本海軍が奇襲攻撃した　₆**World   War   Ⅱ**：第二次世界大戦(1939-45)　₇**Nikkei**：日系人　₁₀**foreigner**：外国人　₁₃**apology**：謝罪
p73→ ₂**enka singer**：演歌歌手 ₄**prove**：証明する ₄**talent**：才能　₄**due to**：〜による ₉**Yokohama Film Festival**：横浜映画祭 ₁₀**fluent**：〜が流暢な ₁₀**French**：フランス語₁₂**overseas**：海外の ₁₃**thriller:**スリラー映画₁₆**confidence**：自信 ₁₆**cultural value**：文化的価値　₁₇**influence**：影響　₁₈**fault**：欠点　₁₉**passionate**：情熱的な、熱狂的な　₁₉**diver**：ダイバー ₂₀**countryside**：田舎、田園地帯 ₂₁**farming**：農業

THE LIVES AND TIMES OF MOVIE STARS

♥ Exercise 17-1 ♥
TF Quiz

以下の文章が本文の内容と合っていれば T 、誤りなら F を記入しなさい。

( ) 1. Youki Kudoh was born in Tokyo in 1971. Her father was a famous rock singer, Hachiro Isawa.

( ) 2. Having such a famous father made it difficult sometimes to prove that her success was due to her own talent, not to her father's name, she said.

( ) 3. She is able to speak not only English but also French.

( ) 4. Her first big hit was in an Australian thriller in 1997. As a result, she is often a public face of Japan to other countries.

( ) 5. She moved for a time to the countryside to spend time farming.

♥ Exercise 17-2 ♥
Japanese to English

以下の日本語の文章を英語に直しなさい。

ある点では、きみの気持ちもわかるけど、まだ僕が正しいと思っている。

_____

読書をして時間を過ごすのが好きだ。

_____

Youki Kudoh

♥ Exercise 17-3 ♥
Structure and Vocabulary

次の空欄に文脈に即した単語を下記から選び記入しなさい。本文の内容が
ヒントになるものもあります。

1. (   ) her parents were born in the United States,
   they were put into camps just as if they were foreigners
   from Japan.

   (A) Even
   (B) Although
   (C) However
   (D) Therefore

2. She is (   ) in French, English and Japanese.
   That's why she became an interpreter.

   (A) fluent
   (B) for
   (C) fool
   (D) fractured

3. She once said in an interview that Japanese need to have
   more (   ) in their own cultural values.

   (A) confide
   (B) confidence
   (C) confidential
   (D) confiding

★18★
Jennifer Lopez

Ricky :Gee, Yumi, how many times do you have to watch the same music video?

Yumi :I'm just trying to get the steps right that Jennifer Lopez does. See, look at her right there - isn't that just so cool?

Ricky :Uh, yeah. You going to do that next time we go out?

Yumi :Well, I can try. You know the saying, "No harm in trying."

Ricky :Go for it, girl. You do that and every guy in the place will want to be me, taking you home at closing time!

Jennifer Lynn Lopez was born in New York in 1969. Her parents encouraged her sisters and her to sing and perform at home to keep them "out of trouble." She started taking singing and dancing lessons when she was five years old. When she was in her last year of high school, she got a small role in a movie. After high school she was in several musicals, performing in Europe and Japan as well as New York. She also appeared in some television shows and had small parts in movies.

By the mid-1990s she started appearing in more and more movies. At the same time, she pursued a singing career, singing in both English and Spanish. Although she is very insecure about her voice, her singing career has been just as successful as her acting career. She has won many awards for both singing and acting.

She says that her children are very important to her. With her sister she has started the Maribel Foundation. This foundation works to help poor mothers get medical help and vaccinations for their children.

---

p76→₁ **gee** :あらまあ、うわー、うっそー ₅ **cool** :かっこいい ₇ **saying** :ことわざ ₇ **No harm in trying**. :だめもとで、やってみたら。(ことわざ) ₉ **go for it** :がんばれ
p77→ ₂ **encourage** :励ます ₃ **perform** :役などを演じる ₆ **role** :役 ₇ **musical** :ミュージカル ₇ **Europe** :ヨーロッパ、欧州 ₆ **several** :いくつかの ₇ **as well as** :〜と同様の ₁₀ **mid-1990s** :1990年代中頃 ₁₀ **appear** :現れる ₁₀ **more and more** :ますます ₁₁ **at the same time** :同時に ₁₁ **pursue** :追求する、続ける ₁₂ **Spanish** :スペイン語 ₁₃ **insecure** :不安定な、こわれやすい ₁₇ **the Maribel Foundation** :マリベル財団・俳優のジェニファーロペスが設立した財団で、貧困な家庭の母親の子供たちに対して医療的な援助を行っている ₁₈ **medical help** : 医療的な援助
₁₉ **vaccination** :ワクチンの予防接種

THE LIVES AND TIMES OF MOVIE STARS

♥ Exercise 18-1 ♥
TF Quiz

以下の文章が本文の内容と合っていれば T 、誤りなら F を記入しなさい。

( ) 1. Jennifer Lynn Lopez was born in the 20th century. Her parents encouraged her sisters and her to sing and perform at home to keep them "out of trouble."

( ) 2. When she was six years old, she had already started taking singing and dancing lessons.

( ) 3. By the mid-1990s her movies were less popular.

( ) 4. She is proud of her voice.

( ) 5. She has won many awards for only singing.

♥ Exercise 18-2 ♥
Japanese to English

以下の日本語の文章を英語に直しなさい。

きみが被っている帽子は、とても格好いいね!

_____

彼は役者の仕事をしたい。

_____

Jennifer Lopez

♥ Exercise 18-3 ♥
Structure and Vocabulary

次の空欄に文脈に即した単語を下記から選び記入しなさい。本文の内容が
ヒントになるものもあります。

1. How much time do you (　　　　　) practicing English
    every day?

    (A) have
    (B) take
    (C) go
    (D) spend

2. By the mid-1990s she started appearing in (　　　　　)
    movies.

    (A) timely
    (B) more and more
    (C) more like
    (D) most

3. The wage gap between rich (　　　　) poor countries
    is expanding dramatically.

    (A) but
    (B) nor
    (C) or
    (D) and

★19★
Marilyn Monroe

Yumi : I was thinking this morning about famous people who die when they are still young.
Ricky : What do you mean?
Yumi : Well, look at Marilyn Monroe. She died when she was only 36, so the only images we have of her are when she was young and beautiful. That's why we still see her picture in advertising or movies.
Ricky : OK...
Yumi : That's so different from actors who live a long life. We have an image of them as young people, but then a very different image as older people. Like Sean Connery.
Ricky : I guess you're right. The ones who die young are kind of immortal.

Marilyn Monroe

Norma Jeane Mortenson was born in 1926 in Los Angeles. She became famous as Marilyn Monroe. Monroe was her mother's maiden name. She had a very difficult childhood. Her mother separated before she was born, and she was never sure who her father was. Her mother had mental and financial problems, so she lived with different foster parents. When she was in middle school, she was attacked by the son of one of her foster families. She married her first husband when she was still a young teenager.

A photographer saw her at work and helped her work with a modeling agency. Because the agency wanted blond models, she began coloring her brown hair blond. She quickly became a successful model. A film director saw her and she started making movies. She was successful in the 1950s and appeared in many movies. She quickly became known as the symbol of American female beauty. But even though she was famous and successful, she had stage fright and had difficulty working in front of a camera or an audience.

She developed problems with sleeping pills and alcohol. She made her last movie in 1960. She died in 1962 from barbiturate poisoning.

---

p80→ 6 **that is why**：そういうわけで　2 **still**：まだ　5 **image**：イメージ　12 **Sean Connery**：スコットランド出身の映画俳優で、『007』シリーズの初代ジェームズボンド役で一躍有名となる。　13 **right**：正しい　14 **immortal**：不滅の

p81→ 3 **maiden name**：旧姓　3 **difficult**：困難な　4 **childhood**：子供時代、児童期　6 **mental**:精神の　6 **financial**:財政的な　7 **foster parent**:里親、養い親　8 **attack**：暴力をふるう、暴行する　9 **marry**：結婚する　11 **photographer**:写真家　12 **modeling agency**:モデルの代理業　12 **blond model**:金髪のモデル　13 **color**:色をつける　14 **film director**：映画監督　17 **symbol**：シンボル　17 **female**：女性の　17 **beauty**：美人　18 **fright**:恐怖　19 **in front of**：〜の前で　21 **sleeping pill**：睡眠薬　21 **alcohol**：アルコール飲料　23 **barbiturate poisoning**：バルビツール酸塩による毒殺

THE LIVES AND TIMES OF MOVIE STARS

♥ Exercise 19-1 ♥

TF Quiz

以下の文章が本文の内容と合っていれば T 、誤りなら F を記入しなさい。

(   )   1. Marilyn Monroe had a very difficult childhood, not knowing who her father was.

(   )   2. She was fostered by only one family.

(   )   3. She got married to her first husband when she was still a teenager.

(   )   4. She became a successful model in the 1950s.

(   )   5. She died in 1962 due to sleeping pill abuse.

♥ Exercise 19-2 ♥

Japanese to English

以下の日本語の文章を英語に直しなさい。

プラハの地下鉄の系統は、われわれのとは大きく異なる。

_____

まだ私たちが学生だった頃に、私はトーマスと結婚した。

_____

Marilyn Monroe

♥ Exercise 19-3 ♥
Structure and Vocabulary

次の空欄に文脈に即した単語を下記から選び記入しなさい。本文の内容が
ヒントになるものもあります。

1. Because the agency wanted blond models, she began coloring her (　　　　　).

    (A) hair to blond
    (B) brown hair blond
    (C) blond hair to brown
    (D) brown to blond hair

2. She quickly became known (　　　　　) the symbol of American female beauty.

    (A) to
    (B) with
    (C) as
    (D) about

3. She died in 1962 (　　　　　) barbiturate poisoning.

    (A) due
    (B) owe to
    (C) because
    (D) from

★20★
Paul Newman

Ricky :I was rummaging around and found these old photos.
Yumi :This photo looks like you were having a lot of fun. When was it taken?
Ricky :That was when I was a student at university. We used to celebrate Newman Day with some pretty wild parties.
Yumi :Newman? Like in Paul Newman?
Ricky :Yeah, it was named after him. But in 2004 he asked us to stop naming it after him. His son died from a drug overdose at a pretty wild party, so he didn't like us to use his name like that.
Yumi :That's easy to understand.

Paul Newman

Paul Leonard Newman was born in 1925 in Ohio, USA. During WWII he wanted to be a pilot, but he couldn't because he was color blind. Instead, he was an ordinary soldier. After the war he studied drama at university in New York City. His first acting was on stage at Broadway. Then he moved to Hollywood to be in movies in the mid-1950s. He was a popular actor for many years and with different generations, especially for his parts as a rebel. He retired from acting in 2007.

Besides his movie career, he started a food company that gave all its profits to charities, including the Hole in the Wall Camps. These are summer camps for thousands of seriously ill children. He also gave millions of dollars of scholarships to university students. Another charity was a drug abuse prevention center that he set up after his own son died from a drug overdose. He was an active supporter of environmental and gay rights issues.

He was also famous for auto racing. This started after he was training for a movie role as a race driver. He continued racing until he was 70 years old. He had smoked heavily for many years and died from lung cancer in 2008.

---

p84→ ₅ **used to**：～したものだった ₅ **celebrate**：祝う ₅ **pretty**：かなり ₈ **name after**：～にちなんで名づける ₁₀ **drug**：薬物 ₁₀ **overdose:**盛りすぎ ₁₀ **wild**：荒っぽい
p85→ ₁ **Ohio**：オハイオ・米国北東部の州で州都は Columbus ₂ **WWⅡ**：World War Ⅱ・第2次世界大戦(1939-45) ₂ **pilot**：パイロット ₃ **color blind**：色盲 ₃ **instead**：代わりに ₃ **ordinary**：普通の ₄ **soldier**：兵士 ₈ **generation:**世代 ₈ **especially**：特に ₈ **rebel:**反逆者、反抗者 ₈ **retire**：引退する ₁₀ **food company**：食料品会社 ₁₁ **profit**：利益 ₁₁ **charity**：慈善 ₁₃ **ill**：病気 ₁₃ **millions of**：何百万もの ₁₃ **scholarship:**奨学金 ₁₄ **drug abuse**：麻薬の乱用 ₁₅ **prevention center**：予防センター ₁₅ **set up**：設立する ₁₆ **supporter**：支持者 ₁₈ **auto racing**：自動車レース ₁₉ **race driver**：レースドライバー ₂₀ **continue**：続ける ₂₀ **smoke**：喫煙する ₂₁ **lung cancer**：肺がん

THE LIVES AND TIMES OF MOVIE STARS

♥ Exercise 20-1 ♥
TF Quiz

以下の文章が本文の内容と合っていれば T、誤りなら F を記入しなさい。

( )　1. Paul Newman was not able to become a pilot because his skin color was black.

( )　2. After the war he studied drama at university and then moved to Hollywood where he became a popular actor.

( )　3. He ran a food company while holding summer camps for seriously ill children all by himself.

( )　4. He was active in a number of fields, such as financial aid for university students, drug abuse prevention, environmental problems and gay rights issues.

( )　5. He was good at auto racing as well as acting.

♥ Exercise 20-2 ♥
Japanese to English

以下の日本語の文章を英語に直しなさい。

それは大変そうに見えるが、実際にはそうではない。

_____

大学に入学した時にはすでに、私は3本の映画に出ていた。

_____

Paul Newman

♥ Exercise 20-3 ♥
Structure and Vocabulary

次の空欄に文脈に即した単語を下記から選び記入しなさい。本文の内容が
ヒントになるものもあります。

1. (   ) he wanted to be a pilot, he couldn't because he was color blind.

   (A) Since

   (B) As long as

   (C) Although

   (D) As if

2. Besides his movie career, he started a food company that gave (   ), including the Hole in the Wall Camps.

   (A) charities to all its profits

   (B) all charities to its profits

   (C) all of the its profits to charities

   (D) all its profits to charities

3. He was also famous (   ) his auto racing.

   (A) for

   (B) to

   (C) in

   (D) on

★21★
Brad Pitt

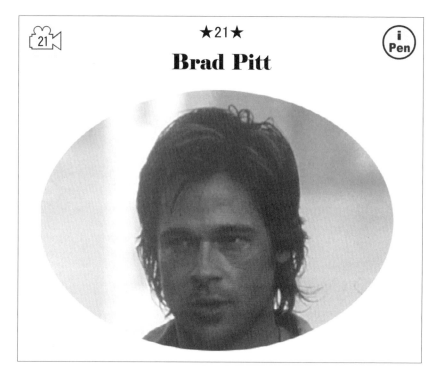

Ricky : I'm glad nobody knows me.

Yumi : What do you mean, "nobody"? Everybody in the neighborhood knows you. They all know what you do and where you go.

Ricky : I mean really famous. Like Brad Pitt and Angelina Jolie. They had to go all the way to Namibia in Africa to have their baby. And even there, people were trying to take pictures of them all the time. If I want to be alone, I don't need to go to Africa. All I have to do is go to the other side of town.

Yumi : Well, you better keep a low profile on the way. Remember Andy Warhol said that everyone has their "15 minutes of fame."

Brad Pitt

William Bradley Pitt was born in Oklahoma in 1963. He grew up in Missouri and was very active in sports when he was young. At university he studied journalism, but he decided to work in films after graduation. He got his first small parts in television programs and films in 1987. He started to get bigger roles in the 1990s. He is now one of the most famous actors in the world. He has been in many different kinds of movies.

Several magazines have called him one of the sexiest men in the world. His personal life has been of interest to many people. This is especially because of his relationship with Angelina Jolie and the birth and adoption of their children.

He is active in projects that support a better life for people in the Third World. He has given much money to groups helping to stop malaria and reduce poverty. He is also interested in making housing better for the environment. He is a strong supporter of gay marriage rights. He says he and the mother of his children will not be married until all people in the United States have the right to marry.

---

p88→ ₃ **neighborhood**：近所　₆ **all the way**：はるばる　₆ **Namibia**：ナミビア・アフリカ南部の国　₈ **all the time**：いつも
p89→₁ **Oklahoma**：オクラホマ・米国中部の州で州都は Oklahoma City　₂ **Missouri**：ミズーリ・米国中部の州で州都 Jefferson City ₃ **journalism**：ジャーナリズム ₄ **graduation**：卒業 ₉ **magazine**：雑誌 ₉ **sexy**：セクシーな ₁₀ **personal**：一個人の ₁₁ **especially:**特に ₁₁ **because of**：〜のために ₁₁ **relationship**：間柄，関係 ₁₂ **birth**：誕生 ₁₂ **adoption**：養子縁組 ₁₃ **active**：活動的な　₁₃ **project**：事業 ₁₄ **the Third World**：第三世界・アジア・アフリカ・中南米など発展途上国 ₁₅ **malaria**：マラリア ₁₅ **reduce**：減らす ₁₅ **poverty**：貧困　₁₆ **environment**：環境　₁₇ **gay marriage right**：同性愛者の結婚の権利

THE LIVES AND TIMES OF MOVIE STARS

♥ Exercise 21-1 ♥
TF Quiz

以下の文章が本文の内容と合っていれば T 、誤りなら F を記入しなさい。

(　　) 1. William Bradley Pitt was born in Oklahoma in 1963. He grew up in Missouri and was very active in sports when he was young.

(　　) 2. His major at university was journalism.

(　　) 3. Several magazines have called him one of the sexiest men in the world.

(　　) 4. His personal life has been of interest to many people. This is especially due to his relationship with Angelina Jolie and the birth and adoption of their children.

(　　) 5. He hates gay marriage.

♥ Exercise 21-2 ♥
Japanese to English

以下の日本語の文章を英語に直しなさい。

どういう意味、イタリア料理が好きじゃないってこと?

_____

彼女は近所で最もかわいい女性の1人だ。

_____

Brad Pitt

♥ Exercise 21-3 ♥
Structure and Vocabulary

次の空欄に文脈に即した単語を下記から選び記入しなさい。本文の内容が
ヒントになるものもあります。

1. At university he (　　　　) in journalism, but he
   decided to work in films after graduation.

   (A) prepare

   (B) prevent

   (C) mean

   (D) majored

2. One of the biggest problems famous actors have is their
   interest to many people, especially (　　　　) they go
   on a vacation.

   (A) whenever

   (B) whatever

   (C) however

   (D) whoever

3. Malaria (　　　　) a bite from an infected female
   mosquito.

   (A) beginning with

   (B) begun

   (C) begins with

   (D) began

★22★
Keanu Reeves

Ricky :Do you know much about dyslexia, Yumi?
Yumi :A bit. In America I had a friend at school who was dyslexic. She was very intelligent, but she couldn't read or write at all. She had a helper to read everything to her, all her textbooks and teachers' notes. She would then tell the helper what to write for homework assignments. She had an amazing memory.
Ricky :Someone told me there's no dyslexia in Japan.
Yumi :That's not true at all. The problem is that many teachers don't know about it, so they just say a student is stupid or lazy.

Keanu Charles Reeves was born in 1964 in Lebanon. His mother was from England and his father from Hawaii. Keanu is a Hawaiian name meaning "coldness." His father left the family when Keanu was three, and he lived in many cities in several countries. He ended up in Canada and is now a Canadian citizen. He had much difficulty in school because of his dyslexia, but he was a very good hockey player. He never finished high school.

He started acting as a child and appeared on stage and in commercials as a teenager. His first movie was a Canadian hockey film. After this he drove to Los Angeles, where he continued acting. Some of his films there were big hits, while others were not until his role in *The Matrix* series. This was a world-wide success.

He is a practicing Buddhist. His long-time girlfriend Jennifer Syme died in 2001 and he has never married. He has had many problems with photographers and journalists who try to disturb his privacy. He has homes in both New York City and the Los Angeles area.

---

p92→ 1 **dyslexic** ：失語症患者　3 **intelligent** ：聡明な　4 **helper** ：協力者　6 **note** ：覚え書、メモ　7 **homework assignment** ：宿題　7 **amazing** ：驚嘆すべき
8 **memory** ：記憶　12 **stupid** ：愚かな　12 **lazy** ：怠惰な
p93→ 1 **Lebanon** ：レバノン・地中海東岸にある共和国で首都は Beirut　3 **coldness** ：寒さ、冷淡　5 **several** ：いくつもの　5 **Canada** ：カナダ・北米大陸北部の国で首都は Ottawa　7 **hockey** ：ホッケー　12 **big hit** ：大ヒット　14 **world-wide** ：世界中の
15 **practicing** ：実践している、活動している　15 **long-time** ：長年の　15 **girlfriend** ：ガールフレンド　17 **photographer** ：カメラマン　17 **journalist** ：ジャーナリスト、報道記者　18 **disturb** ：かき乱す　18 **privacy** ：私生活

THE LIVES AND TIMES OF MOVIE STARS

♥ Exercise 22-1 ♥
TF Quiz

以下の文章が本文の内容と合っていれば T 、誤りなら F を記入しなさい。

(   )   1. The word "keanu" is a Hawaiian word meaning "coldness" in English.

(   )   2. Since his father left the family when he was young, Keanu constantly moved from country to country.

(   )   3. Keanu has Canadian citizenship.

(   )   4. He couldn't graduate from high school because he was physically ill.

(   )   5. It was not until he was in the Matrix series that he became really popular all over the world.

♥ Exercise 22-2 ♥
Japanese to English

以下の日本語の文章を英語に直しなさい。

問題は、ジョンが宿題を提出しないことだ。

_____

ホウコは、「宝の壺」を意味する日本人の名前だ。

_____

Keanu Reeves

♥ Exercise 22-3 ♥
Structure and Vocabulary

次の空欄に文脈に即した単語を下記から選び記入しなさい。本文の内容が
ヒントになるものもあります。

1. After this he drove to Los Angeles (   ) he
   continued acting.

   (A) which

   (B) that

   (C) where

   (D) when

2. This was a world-wide (   ).

   (A) successful

   (B) succeed

   (C) success

   (D) successfully

3. He has had many problems (   ) photographers
   and journalists (   ) try to disturb his privacy.

   (A) with   / who

   (B) with   / they

   (C) about   / they

   (D) in   / who

★23★
Julia Roberts

Ricky :That's an interesting question, whether lawyers should get a lot of money from helping people in trouble. I don't like it.

Yumi :But if they don't help those people take their problems to court, who is going to help them?

Ricky :I know. But the idea that your money all comes from people in trouble doesn't seem right to me. There's a difference between helping people and taking money from them when they are down.

Yumi :But we all do that. I give private lessons to kids who are having problems learning, right? Isn't that the same thing?

Julia Roberts

Julia Fiona Roberts was born in the southern American city of Atlanta in 1967. Her parents were active in theater and ran an acting workshop when she was young. Her parents divorced when she was in elementary school. Soon after, her father died. She wanted to be a veterinarian when she was young, but after high school she went to New York to work in modeling and theater.

When she was still a teenager, she had her first big role in *Satisfaction*. She worked in television as well as movie roles. Since the 1990s she has had a number of roles in successful movies and as a voice actress. She had her first Broadway stage role in 2006, but this was not as successful with critics as her film roles.

She has also produced four movies, all based on a series of books for young girls. The books and movies deal with American history.

She is a strong Hindu. She spends much time and money helping UNICEF. She also works to teach people about Rett syndrome, a serious illness of the nervous system. Today she lives with her husband Daniel Moder and children on her ranch in New Mexico.

---

p96→ ₁ **interesting**：おもしろい ₁ **question**：質問 ₁ **whether**：〜かどうか
₁ **lawyer**：弁護士 ₂ **in trouble**：問題を抱えている ₅ **problem**：問題 ₅ **court**：裁判所 ₁₀ **private lesson**：個人授業 ₁₀ **kid**：子ども
p97→ ₂ **Atlanta**：アトランタ・米国 Georgia 州の州都 ₂ **theater**：劇場
₃ **workshop**：研修会、勉強会 ₅ **veterinarian**：獣医 ₆ **New York**：ニューヨーク・米国 New York 州の南東部にある港市 ₁₁ **voice actress**：女性の声優
₁₂ **Broadway**：ブロードウェイ、米国演劇界の代名詞 ₁₃ **critic**：批評家 ₁₄ **based on**：〜に基づいた ₁₅ **deal with**：〜を取り扱う ₁₆ **American history**：アメリカの歴史
₁₇ **Hindu**：ヒンドゥー教徒 ₁₉ **Rett syndrome**：レット症候群・2歳頃の女児に現れる原因不明の神経変性疾患 ₁₉ **illness**：病気 ₁₉ **nervous system**：神経組織 ₂₁ **New Mexico**：ニューメキシコ・米国南西部の州で、州都は Santa Fe

THE LIVES AND TIMES OF MOVIE STARS

♥ Exercise 23-1 ♥
TF Quiz

以下の文章が本文の内容と合っていれば T、誤りなら F を記入しなさい。

(   ) 1. Atlanta is Julia Roberts's hometown.

(   ) 2. Her parents divorced when she was a child.

(   ) 3. When she was still a teenager, she had her first big role in *Satisfaction*.

(   ) 4. Her first Broadway stage role was in 1990.

(   ) 5. She also works to teach people about Rett syndrome, a serious illness of the nervous system.

♥ Exercise 23-2 ♥
Japanese to English

以下の日本語の文章を英語に直しなさい。

私たちと一緒に映画に行きたいんだよね?

_____

映画の仕事には疲れたから、いつか舞台での役をもらいたい。

_____

Julia Roberts

♥ Exercise 23-3 ♥
Structure and Vocabulary

次の空欄に文脈に即した単語を下記から選び記入しなさい。本文の内容が
ヒントになるものもあります。

1. That's an interesting question, whether lawyers should get a lot of money from helping people (   ).

　　(A) in happiness

　　(B) in common

　　(C) in haste

　　(D) in trouble

2. There is a clear difference between a voice actress (   ) a movie star.

　　(A) or

　　(B) for

　　(C) nor

　　(D) and

3. She has also produced four movies, all based on a series of books for young girls. The books and movies (   ) American history.

　　(A) dealing with

　　(B) deals with

　　(C) deal with

　　(D) deals in

★24★
Arnold Schwarzenegger

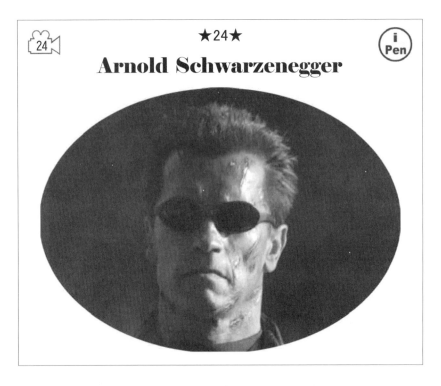

Ricky :I think I'll go to the gym now. Do you want to come along?
Yumi :You exercise too much. It's not healthy to exercise so much.
5 Ricky :What do you mean? What about Arnold Schwarzenegger? He's pretty healthy, isn't he? He was born with a bad heart valve, but he exercises every day, much more than I do. Where did you get the idea that exercise could be bad?
10 Yumi :I just don't think you should overwork your body so much.
Ricky :We were made to have lots of exercise. Sitting around is the most dangerous thing for our bodies.

Arnold Alois Schwarzenegger was born in Austria in 1947. He grew up in a small village. When he was in middle school he started bodybuilding. He started entering bodybuilding competitions when he was seventeen years old. In the 1960s he went to England to train and to learn English. He arrived in the United States when he was twenty-one years old. He spoke English with a strong foreign accent, but he wanted to become a movie star. When he was twenty-three he became the youngest man to win the Mr. Olympia bodybuilding competition.

He started acting in 1970. At first he did not have much success, but in the 1980s, his movies became more and more popular, especially the *Terminator* series. Most of his movies are action films, but he has also been in popular comedy films.

He became an American citizen in 1983 and in 2003 he ran to be governor of California. He won and was also re-elected later. Although he is a member of the conservative Republican party, he has supported many laws to protect the environment.

He continues to be very physically active. In 2004 he even saved a man drowning in the ocean in Hawaii.

---

p100→₁ **gym**：ジム ₂**come along**：一緒に来る ₃ **healthy**：健康な、健全な ₃ **exercise:** 練習する、鍛える ₅ **What do you mean?**：どういう意味なの ₆ **pretty**：かなり ₇ **heart valve**：心臓弁 ₁₀ **overwork**：動かせすぎる ₁₀ **body**：からだ ₁₃ **dangerous**：危険な p101→ ₁ **Austria**：オーストリア・現在は共和国になっているヨーロッパ中部の国で首都は Vienna ₃ **middle school**：中等学校・米国では小学校の高学年と中学校を含む 5-8学年 ₄ **bodybuilding**：ボディービル ₄ **competition**：競技会 ₅ **train**：トレーニングする ₈ **foreign accent**：外国なまり ₈ **movie star**：映画スター ₁₄ **action film**：アクション映画 ₁₅ **comedy film**：コメディー映画 ₁₆ **citizen**：国民 ₁₇ **run**：立候補する ₁₇ **governor of California**：カリフォルニア州知事 ₁₇ **win**：勝つ ₁₈ **re-elect**：再選する ₁₉ **conservative**：保守的な ₁₉ **Republican party**：共和党 ₂₀ **protect**：保護する ₂₁ **physically**：肉体的に ₂₂ **save**：救助する ₂₂ **drown**：おぼれる

THE LIVES AND TIMES OF MOVIE STARS

♥ Exercise 24-1 ♥
TF Quiz

以下の文章が本文の内容と合っていれば T 、誤りなら F を記入しなさい。

( ) 1. Arnold Schwarzenegger was born in Austria, but he moved to the United States.

( ) 2. He started entering bodybuilding competitions when he was seventeen years old.

( ) 3. Becoming a movie star requires perfect English skills.

( ) 4. Most of his movies are comedy films, but he has also been in popular action films.

( ) 5. He ran to be governor of California but he is not an American citizen.

♥ Exercise 24-2 ♥
Japanese to English

以下の日本語の文章を英語に直しなさい。

そのような大金を他国に送るべきだとは、私は思わない。

_____

彼女は環境を守るために大統領選に出馬した。

_____

Arnold Schwarzenegger

♥ Exercise 24-3 ♥
Structure and Vocabulary

次の空欄に文脈に即した単語を下記から選び記入しなさい。本文の内容が
ヒントになるものもあります。

1. Becoming an American citizen is (　　　　) difficult
    than getting a Green Card.

    (A) more

    (B) to

    (C) rather than

    (D) for

2. (　　　　) he is a member of the conservative
    Republican party, he has supported many laws to
    protect the environment.

    (A) Though

    (B) Therefore

    (C) In spite of

    (D) Despite

3. When he was twenty-three he became the youngest man
    to win the Mr. Olympia bodybuilding (　　　　).

    (A) compete

    (B) competition

    (C) competing

    (D) competitive

- 103 -

★25★
Will Smith

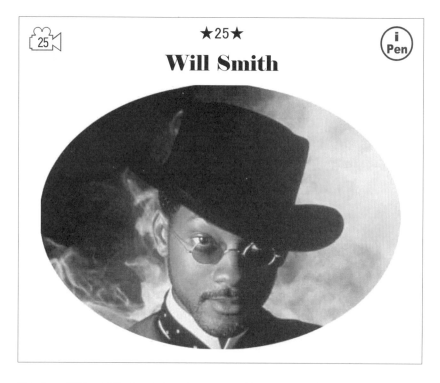

Ricky : What kind of movies did you watch when you were a kid, Yumi?

Yumi : I used to love westerns. Especially the good guys-bad guys kind of western.

Ricky : Me, too. But these days they seem kind of, well, too simple. Know what I mean?

Yumi : I know. The world isn't so simple, not so black-and-white. But I still like movies set in that time and place. Especially comedies.

Ricky : Like *Wild Wild West* with Will Smith?

Yumi : Yeah. A movie like that makes you laugh at all the things we loved as kids in westerns.

Will Smith

Will Smith was born Willard Christopher Smith, Jr in 1968 in the American state of Pennsylvania. Although his mother was a teacher and his father an engineer, he never wanted to go to university. Instead he turned to music and as a young man became a rap singer and song writer.

He was successful, but he did not manage his money well and ended up losing most of it to pay for taxes. Then he was given an acting role in the TV comedy *The Fresh Prince of Bel-Air*. Some years later he got a role in movies, many of which were very successful. He is so famous that President Barack Obama once said that when a film is made about his life, he hopes Will Smith plays him. In recent years he has produced movies as well as acted in them.

Will Smith has a strong interest in different religions, and has donated much money to Christian, Muslim, and Jewish schools and organizations. He and his wife Jada have also started their own elementary school in California.

---

p104→ ₁ **what kind of**：どんな種類の ₂ **kid**：子供 ₃ **especially**：特に ₄ **western**：西部劇 ₆ **simple**：単純 ₈ **black-and-white**：黒白のはっきりした、単純明快な ₉ **comedy**：喜劇 ₁₁ **make one laugh**：人を笑わせる

p105→₂ **Pennsylvania**：the Commonwealth of Pennsylvania・ペンシルベニア・米国東部の州で州都は Harrisburg ₂ **Although**：〜にもかかわらず ₃ **engineer:**エンジニア ₄ **instead**：その代わりに₅ **rap singer**：ラップ歌手₅ **song writer**：作曲家 ₆ **successful**：成功した ₆ **manage**：管理する ₇ **tax**：税金 ₈ **TV comedy**：テレビのコメディ番組 ₉ **some years later**：数年後に ₉ **get a role**：配役を得る ₁₁ **President Barack Obama**：アメリカ合衆国の第44代大統領 ₁₂ **hope**：希望する ₁₂ **play**：演じる ₁₂ **in recent years**：近年 ₁₃ **produce**：制作する ₁₃ **as well as**：〜と同様に ₁₄ **interest**：関心 ₁₄ **religion**：宗教 ₁₅ **donate**：寄付する ₁₅ **Christian**：キリスト教徒の ₁₅ **Muslim**：イスラム教徒の ₁₅ **Jewish**：ユダヤ教徒の ₁₆ **school**：学校 ₁₆ **organization**：機関 ₁₇ **elementary school**：小学校 ₁₇ **California**：カリフォルニア・米国太平洋岸の州で、州都は Sacramento

THE LIVES AND TIMES OF MOVIE STARS

♥ Exercise 25-1 ♥
TF Quiz

以下の文章が本文の内容と合っていれば T 、誤りなら F を記入しなさい。

(　) 1. Will Smith never wanted to go to college, although his parents are highly educated people.

(　) 2. He was a rock singer.

(　) 3. He went into bankruptcy.

(　) 4. Barack Obama once said that when a film is made about his life, he hopes Will Smith plays him.

(　) 5. He is interested in different religions.

♥ Exercise 25-2 ♥
Japanese to English

以下の日本語の文章を英語に直しなさい。

彼女はいつも単純明快な考え方をする。

_____

誰があの映画で魔女を演じているの?

_____

Will Smith

♥ Exercise 25-3 ♥
Structure and Vocabulary

次の空欄に文脈に即した単語を下記から選び記入しなさい。本文の内容が
ヒントになるものもあります。

1. (   ) his mother being a teacher and his father an
   engineer, he never wanted to go to university.

   (A) Despite
   (B) Though
   (C) In spite of
   (D) Because of

2. He was successful, but he did not (   ) his
   money well and ended up losing most of it to pay for
   taxes.

   (A) waste
   (B) get
   (C) drive
   (D) manage

3. He did charitable work about religions. (   ), he
   has donated much money to Christian, Muslim, and
   Jewish schools and organizations.

   (A) However
   (B) For instance
   (C) But
   (D) For gain

- 107 -

THE LIVES AND TIMES OF MOVIE STARS

★26★
Sylvester Stallone

Ricky :Hi Yumi. Want to go out and have an ice cream or something?

Yumi :Sorry, Ricky, I'm on my way to the gym.

Ricky :The gym? I didn't know you were working out. Taking an aerobics class or something?

Yumi :No, boxing.

Ricky :Boxing? No way! You'll get hurt.

Yumi :Not with protective clothing. And my teacher shows us how not to be hurt. It's a great way to get fit. You should come, too.

Ricky :No way! You'd beat me up and knock me out. I'll stick with the ice cream.

- 108 -

Michael Sylvester Gardenzio Stallone was born in New York City in 1946. Because of problems at his birth, a nerve in his face was cut, so part of his face is paralyzed and his speech has always been a little unclear. When he was young, his parents had problems in their marriage, so he lived with other families. He ended up living with his mother after they divorced. He went to a military high school.

As a young man he was homeless for a while, sleeping in a bus station. During this time he had his first acting role, in a pornographic movie and then in an erotic play on stage.

Later he was able to get more normal roles. He became famous as Rocky. He actually wrote the script for *Rocky* himself after watching a fight with Muhammad Ali.

He won several Academy Awards for the series of ten movies. These and many of his other films were especially popular outside the United States. He does most of his own stunts in these movies, and as a result, has been injured many times as an actor.

---

p108→ ₁**go out**：外出する ₁**ice cream**：アイスクリーム ₃**on my way to**：〜へ行く途中で ₅**aerobics class**：エアロビの授業 ₆**boxing**：ボクシング ₇**no way**：馬鹿げている、まさか ₈**protective clothing**：保護服 ₁₉**hurt**：傷つける ₁₁**beat**：続けざまに打つ ₁₁**knock**：ゴツンと打つ ₁₂**stick with**：〜を手放さないでいる
p109→₂**problem**：問題 ₂**nerve**：神経 ₃**paralyze**：麻痺する ₄**speech**：スピーチ、話 ₅**marriage**：結婚 ₇**military**：軍隊の ₈**homeless**：ホームレスの ₈**for a while**：しばらくの間 ₁₀**pornographic movie**：ポルノ映画 ₁₀**erotic play**：官能的な演技 ₁₀**on stage**：舞台で ₁₁**normal**：ふつうの ₁₂**script**：台本、脚本 ₁₃**Muhammad Ali**：モハメッド・アリ・プロボクサーで元世界ヘビー級チャンピオン。パーキンソン病にかかり、闘病生活を送っている ₁₅**especially**：特に ₁₇**stunt**：スタント ₁₇**injure**：傷つける

THE LIVES AND TIMES OF MOVIE STARS

♥ Exercise 26-1 ♥
TF Quiz

以下の文章が本文の内容と合っていれば T 、誤りなら F を記入しなさい。

( ) 1. Sylvester Stallone is from Buffalo in New York State.

( ) 2. His speech has been always unclear because part of his face is paralyzed.

( ) 3. When he was a young man, he was richer than his parents.

( ) 4. He had his first acting role in a pornographic movie and then in an erotic play on stage.

( ) 5. Many of his films were only popular inside the US.

♥ Exercise 26-2 ♥
Japanese to English

以下の日本語の文章を英語に直しなさい。

今、病院に行く途中の車の中にいる。

_____

10代のころ、私は学校で多くの問題を抱えていた。

_____

- 110 -

Sylvester Stallone

♥ Exercise 26-3 ♥
Structure and Vocabulary

次の空欄に文脈に即した単語を下記から選び記入しなさい。本文の内容が
ヒントになるものもあります。

1. The massive snow storm (   ) the public
    transportation.

    (A) paralyzed

    (B) promoted

    (C) encouraged

    (D) kept

2. In developing countries, there are many families who
    (   ) problems getting enough food.

    (A) had

    (B) have

    (C) has

    (D) having

3. He does most of his own stunts in these movies;
    (   ), he has been injured many times as an
    actor.

    (A) anymore

    (B) inevitably

    (C) therefore

    (D) however

★27★
Sharon Stone

Ricky :If you could buy a memory that was fake, what memory would you buy?

Yumi :You mean like in *Total Recall?*

Ricky :Yeah. You get a shot and then think the memory was real.

Yumi :I don't think I would like that. I would never know if my memory was real or not. And our lives are really just our memories. I'd hate to mess up the great ones I've had. What about you?

Ricky :You know how I am afraid of water. I would like a memory of swimming in the open ocean. Maybe then I would not be afraid to go swimming.

Sharon Stone

Sharon Vonne Stone was born in Pennsylvania in the eastern United States in 1958. As a teenager she was in beauty contests and so she decided to move to New York City to become a fashion model. She decided to become an actress when she was modeling in Europe, so she moved back to New York. At first she had only very small roles, but in 1984 she began to get bigger parts. Some of her earlier films had nudity. Later she said she was tricked into some of these. Nevertheless, she became a popular actress and many of her films were successful.

In 2001 she had to go to the hospital for a broken artery. After this she made a commercial to help teach people about strokes. She has also raised money for malaria prevention in Tanzania. After the 2008 Sichuan earthquake in China, she made comments against the Chinese government and its attitude against the Dalai Lama. This has meant that she can now no longer work in China.

She is now divorced with three adopted sons.

---

p112→ ₁ **fake**：偽の　₂ **memory**：記憶　　₄ **shot**：推量　　₆ **never**：決して～ない
₁₁ **swimming**：スイミング　₁₁ **open ocean**：外洋　₁₁ **maybe**：ひょっとしたら
p113→₁ **Pennsylvania**：the Commonwealth of Pennsylvania・ペンシルベニア.米国
東部の州で州都 Harrisburg　₂ **eastern**：東部の₃ **decide**：決心する　₃ **move**：移動す
る₈ **nudity**：裸むき出しの状態₈ **trick**：だます、かつぐ₉ **nevertheless**：それでもやは
り₁₀ **successful**：成功した₁₁ **hospital**：病院₁₁ **artery**：動脈₁₃ **stroke**：脳卒中
₁₃ **malaria prevention**：マラリア予防₁₄ **Tanzania**：タンザニア・アフリカ中東部の共和
国₁₄ **Sichuan**：中国の四川省　₁₄ **earthquake**：地震　₁₅ **comment**：批評　₁₅ **Chinese
government**：中国政府　₁₆ **attitude**：態度　₁₆ **against**：～に反して　₁₆ **the Dalai
Lama**：チベット仏教で最上位に位置する化身ラマの名跡で、ここではダライラマ14
世のこと₁₇ **no longer**：もはや～ない₁₈ **divorce**：離婚する₁₈ **adopted**：養子になった

THE LIVES AND TIMES OF MOVIE STARS

♥ Exercise 27-1 ♥
TF Quiz

以下の文章が本文の内容と合っていれば T 、誤りなら F を記入しなさい。

( ) 1. Sharon Stone was born in Pennsylvania in the mid-twentieth century.

( ) 2. When she was a teenager she moved to Europe, where she decided to become a model.

( ) 3. She was a successful actress from the beginning.

( ) 4. She was an active supporter for malaria prevention in Tanzania.

( ) 5. She adopted three sons.

♥ Exercise 29-2 ♥
Japanese to English

以下の日本語の文章を英語に直しなさい。

私は本当に蜘蛛が怖い。

_____

彼はもはや舞台では演じられない。

_____

- 114 -

Sharon Stone

♥ Exercise 27-3 ♥
Structure and Vocabulary

次の空欄に文脈に即した単語を下記から選び記入しなさい。本文の内容が
ヒントになるものもあります。

1. (   ) a teenager she was in beauty contests and
   so she decided to move to New York City to become a
   fashion model.

   (A) When

   (B) As

   (C) At

   (D) On

2. At first she had only very small roles but in 1984 she
   began to get bigger (   ).

   (A) role

   (B) one

   (C) parts

   (D) things

3. This has meant that she can now (   )
   work in China.

   (A) any more

   (B) no longer

   (C) be able to

   (D) not

- 115 -

★28★
Ken Takakura

Yumi :Ricky, why did you pretend that you couldn't speak Japanese just now? Those were your neighbors, the Shimizus.

Ricky :I just don't like them. They are so annoyingly nosey. They always want to know everyone's business. The whole neighborhood doesn't like speaking with them. So I just pretend like I can't speak Japanese.

Yumi :So you left me to talk with them all by myself. And to answer all the questions they wanted to ask you.

Ricky :Yeah, and did you have to tell them so much? Now it'll be spread all over the neighborhood!

Gouichi Oda was born in 1931 in Kyushu, Japan. He later became known as the actor Ken Takakura. As a junior high school student, he loved to learn English. One of his best friends was the son of an American Navy officer. He studied at Meiji University and became a manager in a trading company. In 1955 a friend arranged for him to have an interview for a film. He was an instant success. He played in many Japanese films. In these early films he usually played the part of a tough gangster, but later he played more ordinary characters as well.

In the 1970s he played in several Hollywood films. One of his best known English-language roles was a Japanese police chief in *Black Rain* who speaks English, but hides it from the American police officers he is supposed to be working with. Even though he was popular with American audiences, he kept on making Japanese films.

Now in his eighties, he continues to make movies, although not as many as before. In one of his latest movies he worked with Chinese director Yimou Zhang.

---

p116→　₁ **pretend**：〜のふりをする　₂ **Japanese**：日本語　₂ **neighbor**：隣人
₃ **the Shimizus**：清水家　₄ **annoying**：いやな　₄ **nosey**：詮索好きな　₆ **whole**
：すべての　₆ **neighborhood**：近所　₁₁ **spread**：広げる
p117→　₄ **Navy**：海軍　₄ **officer**：将校　₅ **manager**：経営者、部長　₆ **trading company**：貿易会社　₆ **arrange**：整える、取り決める　₇ **interview**：面接、インタビュー　₇ **instant**：即時　₇ **success**：成功　₉ **usually**：たいてい　₉ **tough**：丈夫な
₉ **gangster**：暴力団員　　₁₀ **ordinary**：通常の　　₁₀ **character**：登場人物、配役
₁₁ **Hollywood**：ハリウッド・米国 Los　Angeles の北西部にある映画製作の中心地。転じて米国の映画界のことも意味する　₁₃ **hide**：隠す　₁₅ **audience**：聴衆、観衆　₁₇ **in his eighties**：80歳代で　₁₉ **director**：監督　₁₉ **Chinese**：中国人の　₁₉ **Yimou Zhang**：張芸謀。中国人の映画監督。俳優やプロデューサー業もこなす。

THE LIVES AND TIMES OF MOVIE STARS

♥ Exercise 28-1 ♥
TF Quiz

以下の文章が本文の内容と合っていれば T 、誤りなら F を記入しなさい。

(   )   1. Ken Takakura is a screen name.

(   )   2. When he was a high school student, he hated to learn foreign languages such as English.

(   )   3. In his early films, he usually played the part of a tough gangster, but later he played more ordinary characters as well.

(   )   4. All his films are made in Japan.

(   )   5. Because he was popular with American audiences, he stopped making Japanese films.

♥ Exercise 28-2 ♥
Japanese to English

以下の日本語の文章を英語に直しなさい。

彼はお金持ちのふりをするのが好きだ。

_____

彼女は70代だが、とても若く見える。

_____

- 118 -

Ken Takakura

♥ Exercise 28-3 ♥
Structure and Vocabulary

次の空欄に文脈に即した単語を下記から選び記入しなさい。本文の内容が
ヒントになるものもあります。

1. (　　　　　) his best friends was the son of an American
   Navy officer.

   (A) Many of
   (B) One of
   (C) Most of
   (D) Many

2. In one of his (　　　　　) movies he worked with
   Chinese director Yimou Zhang.

   (A) later
   (B) lately
   (C) late
   (D) latest

3. Now in his eighties, he continues to make movies,
   (　　　　　) not as many as before.

   (A) for
   (B) thus
   (C) nevertheless
   (D) however

★29★
Robin Williams

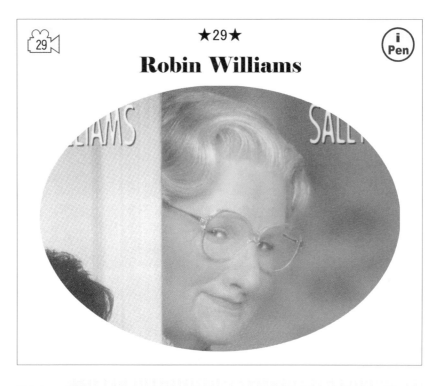

Ricky :I just got an email from my old friend Jack. He is getting a divorce.

Yumi :Oh, that's too bad. He really likes being with his children. Now he'll never be able to see them.

Ricky :What do you mean?

Yumi :Well, you said they're getting a divorce, right? The kids will be with their mother and he won't get to see them.

Ricky :Not in Hawaii. They will probably have joint custody. That means they live with one parent part of the week, and with the other parent the other part of the week.

Robin Williams

Robin McLaurin Williams was born in Chicago in 1951. He was a very shy child. He used high school drama to overcome his shyness. After high school he studied at the famous Juilliard School in New York.

In the 1970s he got his first roles in television comedies where he could use his talent for improvisation and imitating dialects. His films have been very popular. Most of his films are comedies, but he has also been in dramatic films. He won an Oscar in 1998. Many of his early successful films were with Disney, but for many years he had strong disagreements with Disney over marketing and budget cuts. These problems were not solved until 2009.

Although he has had professional success, he also had problems with alcohol and drug addiction. He has spoken publicly about his struggle to overcome drugs after his first child was born.

He often gives time to work with charities. In his free time he also enjoys playing video games. His children were even named after video game characters. Today he lives with his family in California.

---

p120→ ₁ **email**：E メール ₂ **divorce**：離婚 ₃ **that's too bad**．：お気の毒に。
₄ **be able to**：～できる ₉ **joint custody**：離婚（別居）夫婦による連帯保護義務および権利

p121→ ₁ **Chicago**：シカゴ・ Illinois 州 Michigan 湖畔にある米国第3の都市 ₂ **shy**：内気な ₃ **overcome**：打ち勝つ ₃ **shyness**：内気 ₄ **Juilliard School**：ジュリアード学院・ニューヨーク市にある私立の有名な学校で、音楽部門、舞踏部門、演劇部門から成り立つ。 ₆ **talent**：才能 ₆ **improvisation**：即興 ₆ **imitate**：真似る
₇ **dialect**：方言 ₈ **dramatic film**：劇的な映画 ₁₀ **Disney**：ウォルトディズニー社・米国の映画・動画制作社 ₁₁ **disagreement**：不一致 ₁₁ **marketing**：市場戦略・マーケッティング ₁₂ **budget cut**：予算削減 ₁₂ **solve**：解決する ₁₃ **professional success**：プロとしての成功

- 121 -

THE LIVES AND TIMES OF MOVIE STARS

♥ Exercise 29-1 ♥
TF Quiz

以下の文章が本文の内容と合っていれば T 、誤りなら F を記入しなさい。

( ) 1. Robin Williams was too shy to study drama at high school.

( ) 2. He has been in dramatic as well as comedy films.

( ) 3. He won an Oscar in the late 20th century.

( ) 4. He overcame drugs after his first child was born.

( ) 5. Since he is fond of playing video games, his children's names stem from video game characters.

♥ Exercise 29-2 ♥
Japanese to English

以下の日本語の文章を英語に直しなさい。

私の姉と彼女の夫は、離婚するだろう。

_____

私の息子は、ペットと遊ぶことが本当に好きだ。

_____

Robin Williams

♥ Exercise 29-3 ♥
Structure and Vocabulary

次の空欄に文脈に即した単語を下記から選び記入しなさい。本文の内容が
ヒントになるものもあります。

1. (   ) are comedies, but he has also
    been in dramatic films.

    (A) Many his films
    (B) Most of the his films
    (C) Many of the his films
    (D) Most of his films

2. It was (   ) 2009 that these problems (   )
    solved.

    (A) until   / were not
    (B) not until   / were
    (C) until   / were
    (D) not until   / were not

3. His children were even named (   ) video
    game characters.

    (A) for
    (B) after
    (C) before
    (D) of

- 123 -

★30★
Bruce Willis

Ricky :Hi Yumi, what're you doing?
Yumi :Playing my favorite video game.
Ricky :Don't tell me, *Apocalypse*, right? Again, right?
Yumi :Yeah, you know me ….
Ricky :I don't know why you like that old game.
Yumi :Well, you know I just love Bruce Willis. And this was the first time any actor was digitally re-made and put into a video game. It's like being inside your favorite actor's head. I've been playing it since I was a kid.
Ricky :Well, enjoy. I'm going to go out and go jogging. See you.

Bruce Willis

Walter Bruce Willis was born in Germany in 1955. He moved with his family to the United States when he was very young. In high school he became interested in acting to help overcome his problem with stuttering. He started studying acting at university, but never finished.　His first acting roles were in New York plays. Then he got his first role in　the television series *Moonlighting*. Since then he has become one of the world's most financially successful actors.

He is famous for his shaved head and action-hero image. Although he has won many awards for his acting and many of his films are extremely popular, some others have not been so popular. He has also tried performing as a musician, but this has not been as successful as his acting career.

He is interested in politics and supports many conservative political ideas.　He is also a strong supporter of the United States military and its invasion of Iraq. He is also a strong supporter of Israel. He is famous for his very direct way of speaking about his opinions in public.

---

p124→　2 **favorite** ：お気に入りの、大好きな　　2 **video game** ：テレビゲーム
3 **Apocalypse** ：プレイステーション用のテレビゲーム。　　7 **digitally** ：デジタル方式で
7 **re-made** ：再映画化された　　11 **jog** ：ジョギングする
p125→1**Germany** : the Federal Republic of Germany ・ドイツ、首都 Berlin 3 **become interested in** ：～に興味を持つようになる 4 **overcome** ：打ち勝つ、克服する 4 **stutter** ：どもる 8 **financially** ：財政的に 9 **shaved　head** ：そり落とした頭 9 **action-hero** ：アクションヒーロー 9 **image** ：イメージ 11 **extremely** ：すごく 12 **musician** ：音楽家、演奏家
14 **politics** ：政治 14 **conservative** ：保守の 16 **military** ：軍隊 16 **invasion** ：侵入、進出
16 **Iraq** ：イラク・アジア南西部の共和国で首都は Baghdad　17 **Israel** : the State of Israel ・イスラエル・1948年にユダヤ人によって建設された国で、首都は Jerusalem

THE LIVES AND TIMES OF MOVIE STARS

♥ Exercise 30-1 ♥
TF Quiz

以下の文章が本文の内容と合っていれば T 、誤りなら F を記入しなさい。

( ) 1. Bruce Willis moved with his family to the United States as he was very young.

( ) 2. He started studying acting at high school.

( ) 3. He is famous for his shaved head and action-hero image.

( ) 4. His try at performing as a musician was completely successful.

( ) 5. He is a strong supporter of the United States military and its invasion of Iraq.

♥ Exercise 30-2 ♥
Japanese to English

以下の日本語の文章を英語に直しなさい。

彼がきみをデートに誘ったなんて言わないでね!

_____

私たちは政治に興味がない。

_____

Bruce Willis

♥ Exercise 30-3 ♥
Structure and Vocabulary

次の空欄に文脈に即した単語を下記から選び記入しなさい。本文の内容が
ヒントになるものもあります。

1. In high school he became interested in acting to help
    (   ) his problem with stuttering.

    (A) overcoming

    (B) overcome

    (C) overcame

    (D) overcomes

2. Since then he has become one of (   )
    financially successful actors.

    (A) most

    (B) world's most

    (C) the world's more

    (D) the world's most

3. He is famous for his very direct way of speaking about
    his opinions (   ).

    (A) at public

    (B) on public

    (C) in public

    (D) into public

- 127 -

iPen の案内

iPen とは？
- **i**（わたしの）**Pen**（ペン）は内蔵音声データを再生する機器です。
- 先端に赤外線読み取り装置が組み込まれており、ドットコードを読み取ります。
- 上部にスピーカーとマイクロフォンが付いています。

読んでる時が聞きたい瞬間
- 特殊加工（ドットコード）印刷された英文にペン先を当てると、
- スキャナーがドット番号を読み取り内部のシステムを介して…
- MicroSD 内データを呼び出し、音声を再生します。

早送りも巻き戻しも必要なし
- 聞きたいセリフ箇所にペン先を当てるだけで直ちに聞こえます。
- DVD・ブルーレイ・USB など映画ソフト、プレイヤー・パソコンなどハードは必要なし。
- 面倒なチャプター探し、早送り、巻き戻しも一切不要です。

その他の機能紹介

用途	音声録音	USB 対応	ヘッドホンと MicroSD 対応
内容	本体内部にはデジタルメモリーが内蔵されており、本体上部のマイクにより外部（あなたの）音声を一時的に録音させることができます。また、録音音声をドットコードとリンクさせ、再生させることもできます。	付属の USB ケーブルを使用してパソコンと接続することができますから、パソコンで音声データ編集が可能です。単語毎、文章毎、画像の音声化などあなたの用途に応じてさまざまな音声編集をすることができます。	本体には一般ヘッドホンが接続できます。使い慣れたヘッドホンで周囲の環境を気にすることなく本体をご使用いただけます。また、iPen 音声データは基本的に MicroSD カード（別売り）に保存してご利用いただけます。
実用例	シャドーイング学習・発音確認	音声カードやフラッシュカード作り	通動通学学習

iPen の使い方 ①

音声を再生する

電源ボタンで *iPen* を ON にします。（OFF も同様です）

❶ セリフ毎の音声再生
スクリーンプレイの英語文字周辺にペン先をあわせると、印刷行の区切りまで音声を再生することができます。同一人物のセリフでも、長いセリフは途中で分割されています。
繰り返し聞きたいときは、再度、ペン先をあわせます。

❷ チャプター毎の音声再生
チャプター毎にまとめて、連続してセリフを聞きたい時は、スクリーンプレイの目次や各ページに印刷されている 🔘 (DVD) チャプター番号にペン先をあわせます。

❸ スクリーンプレイの目次
スクリーンプレイの目次は今後とも原則「10」で編集しますが、日本発売の標準的 DVD チャプターの区切りに準じます。

iPen 音声データのコピー（移動）

iPen では任意の MicroSD で PC と双方向に *iPen* 音声データのコピーができます。だから、MicroSD は一枚でも結構です。各映画の *iPen* 音声データは PC のフォルダーに保存しておきましょう。

❶ iPen 音声データをダウンロードします
必要な *iPen* 音声データを PC 内フォルダーにダウンロードします。

❷ *iPen* と PC を接続します
iPen 電源オフで付属 USB ケーブルを PC に接続します。

❸ *iPen* 音声データをコピーします
PC 内の *iPen* 音声データを *iPen* の所定フォルダーにコピーします。

❹ 「所定フォルダー」や切断方法など
iPen の所定フォルダーや PC との切断方法など、詳しい内容は *iPen* 付属の取扱説明書をご覧ください。

スクリーンプレイから「音」が出る新時代

主な仕様

製品名	スクリーンプレイ iPen	製造元	Gridmark Inc.型番GT-16010J
サイズ	145×25×21mm	保証期間	購入日より6ヶ月製造元にて
重量	約40グラム	配給元	株式会社FICP
マイク	モノラル	商標	iPenはFICPの登録商標
音声出力	モノラル100mW/8Ω	媒体	MicroSDカード
使用電池	リチウムイオン電池3.7v (400mAh)	音声	専用音声データ（別売り）
充電時間	約5時間（フル充電で約2時間動作）	印刷物	ドットコード付き書籍（別売り）
外部電源	5V/0.8A	動作温度	0～40℃

（詳しくは本体説明書をご覧ください。）

Screenplay「リスニングCD」は？

・「リスニングCD」は、お客様のご要望により当社iPenをご利用されていない学習者の方々のために販売を継続しています。
・「リスニングCD」の有無は、下記のホームページでご確認ください。（パブリックドメイン作品を除きます。）
詳しくはホームページをご覧ください。
https://www.screenplay.jp

入手方法

2019年8月現在、書籍とiPen（2GB以上、MicroSDカード装着済み）は書店でご注文いただけますが、iPen音声データは当社への直接注文に限ります。
下記までご連絡ください。

郵便、電話、FAX、メール、ホームページ

株式会社フォーイン　スクリーンプレイ事業部
〒464-0025　名古屋市千種区桜が丘292
TEL：(052)789-1255　FAX：(052)789-1254
メール：info@screenplay.jp

ネットで注文

https://www.screenplay.jp/ をご覧ください。
（以下の価格表示は2019年8月現在のものです）

iPenの価格

スクリーンプレイ iPen　一台　8,800円（本体価格）
（MicroSDカード「2GB」以上、一枚、装着済み）
（当社発売ドット出版物すべてに共通使用できます）

専用書籍

iPen を使用するには、専用の別売り ドットコード印刷物と iPen 音声データが必要です。
ドット付き　新作　　　スクリーンプレイ　1,600円（本体価格）
ドット付き　クラシック　スクリーンプレイ　1,400円（本体価格）
ドット付き　その他の出版物　表示をご覧ください。

MicroSDカード

iPen 装着以外の MicroSD カードは電気店・カメラ店などでご購入ください。推奨容量は「4GB」以上です。

iPen音声データ（ダウンロード）

iPen音声データ(1タイトルDL)　標準　1,200円（本体価格）
（音声はクラシック・スクリーンプレイシリーズは映画の声、それ以外はネイティブ・スピーカーの録音音声です）

送料

iPen音声データのダウンロード以外は送料が必要です。ホームページをご覧いただくか、当社営業部までお問い合わせください。

iPenの使い方②

音声を録音する	音声をリンクする
❶ 録音モードに切り替える 待機状態で「○ボタン」を2秒以上長押ししてください。LED（左）が赤く点灯し【録音モード】になります。 ❷ 録音する 【録音モード】になったら「○ボタン」を離してください。すぐに録音が開始されます。 ❸ 録音の一時中止 録音中に「○ボタン」を押すと録音を一時停止します。もう一度「○ボタン」を押すと録音を再開します。 ❹ 録音を終了する 「□ボタン」を押すと録音を終了します。 ❺ 録音を消去する 【一部消去】、【全消去】とともに説明書をご覧ください。	リンクとは録音音声をスクリーンプレイ左ページ最下段に印刷された ㊙マーク（空き番号）にリンクすることです。㊙マークにペン先をあわせると録音音声が聞こえるようになります。 ❶【リンクモード】に切り替える リンクしたい音声を選択し、その音声の再生中／録音中／一時停止中に「△ボタン」を2秒以上長押ししてください。LED（左）が橙に点灯し【リンクモード】になります。 ❷ リンクを実行する 【リンクモード】になったら、「△ボタン」を放してください。リンクの確認メッセージが流れます。その後、㊙マークにタッチするとリンク音が鳴り、リンクが完了します。 ❸ リンクを解除する 【一部解除】、【全解除】、その他、説明書をご覧ください。

出版物のご案内 ― 最新情報はホームページをご覧ください

アバウト・タイム　iPen対応

父から譲り受けたタイムトラベルの能力を使ってティムは日々の失敗をやり直す。そして見つけた人生の秘訣とは。
中級
1,600円（本体価格）
四六判変形 208ページ
【978-4-89407-562-7】

雨に唄えば　iPen対応

サイレント映画からトーキー映画の移行期を描いたミュージカル映画の傑作！
初級
1,400円（本体価格）
四六判変形 168ページ
【978-4-89407-548-1】

英国王のスピーチ　iPen対応

幼い頃から吃音という発音障害に悩まされている英国王と一般人スピーチセラピストとの友情を描いた感動作。
中級
1,600円（本体価格）
四六判変形 168ページ
【978-4-89407-473-6】

オズの魔法使　iPen対応

ドロシーと愛犬トトはカンザスで竜巻に巻き込まれ、オズの国マンチキンに迷い込んでしまう。
初級
1,400円（本体価格）
四六判変形 168ページ
【978-4-89407-469-9】

グレース・オブ・モナコ　iPen対応

世紀の結婚から6年、グレース・ケリーと夫、モナコ公国大公は、外交面と夫婦関係で問題を抱えていた。
中級
1,600円（本体価格）
四六判変形 176ページ
【978-4-89407-541-2】

幸せになるための27のドレス　iPen対応
花嫁付き添い人として奔走するジェーン。新聞記者のケビンは、取材先で出会った彼女をネタに記事を書こうと画策する。
中級
1,600円（本体価格）
四六判変形 200ページ
【978-4-89407-471-2】

市民ケーン　iPen対応

かつての新聞王ケーンが死に際に残した謎の言葉「バラのつぼみ」をめぐって物語は進んでいく…。
中級
1,400円（本体価格）
四六判変形 200ページ
【978-4-89407-492-7】

シャーロック 忌まわしき花嫁　iPen対応

B・カンバーバッチ、M・フリーマン主演、大人気海外ドラマ『SHERLOCK』初のスピンオフ映画。
上級
1,600円（本体価格）
四六判変形 184ページ
【978-4-89407-584-9】

シャレード　iPen対応

パリを舞台に、夫の遺産を巡って繰り広げられるロマンチックなサスペンス。
中級
1,400円（本体価格）
四六判変形 228ページ
【978-4-89407-546-7】

ショーシャンクの空に　iPen対応

妻殺害容疑で終身刑に服するアンディー。無罪を主張するも絶望的な状況下、ただ一人「希望」への路を削りゆく。
上級
1,600円（本体価格）
四六判変形 184ページ
【978-4-89407-555-9】

紳士協定　iPen対応

反ユダヤ主義に関する記事の執筆を依頼されたフィルは、ユダヤ人と偽って調査するが、予想以上の差別や偏見を受ける。
上級
1,400円（本体価格）
四六判変形 208ページ
【978-4-89407-522-1】

紳士は金髪がお好き　iPen対応
ダイヤモンドのティアラを巡って起こる大騒動。マリリン・モンローのチャーミングな魅力が満載のミュージカルコメディ。
中級
1,400円（本体価格）
四六判変形 208ページ
【978-4-89407-538-2】

スタンド・バイ・ミー　iPen対応

不良グループの話しを盗み聞きし、目当ての死体を探し旅に出る4人の少年達。最初に見つけてヒーローになろうとするが…。
中級
1,600円（本体価格）
四六判変形 152ページ
【978-4-89407-504-7】

素晴らしき哉、人生！　iPen対応

クリスマス前日、資金繰りに刺し自殺を考えるジョージに、二級天使クラレンスは彼を助けようと…。
中級
1,400円（本体価格）
四六判変形 224ページ
【978-4-89407-497-2】

ダークナイト　iPen対応

新生バットマン・シリーズ第2作。最凶の犯罪者ジョーカーとバットマンの終わりなき戦いが今始まる…。
中級
1,600円（本体価格）
四六判変形 208ページ
【978-4-89407-468-2】

出版物のご案内　　　　　　　　　　　　　価格表示のないものは 1,200 円（本体価格）

食べて、祈って、恋をして　iPen対応

忙しい日々を送り、人生の意味を考え始めたリズが、夫と離婚して、自分探しの3カ国旅に出ることに。
【上級】
1,600 円（本体価格）
四六判変形 192 ページ
【978-4-89407-527-6】

ニュースの真相　iPen対応

二大オスカー俳優が、自らの信念を貫くジャーナリストを演じ、「報道の在り方」を観る者に問いかける骨太な名作。
【上級】
1,600 円（本体価格）
四六判変形 240 ページ
【978-4-89407-594-8】

ノッティングヒルの恋人　iPen対応

ハリウッドの人気女優アナが恋におちたのは、英国で書店を営むウィリアム。住む世界が全く違う二人の恋は前途多難で…。
【中級】
1,600 円（本体価格）
四六判変形 192 ページ
【978-4-89407-570-2】

バック・トゥ・ザ・フューチャー　iPen対応

高校生のマーティは30年前にタイム・スリップし、若き日の両親のキューピットに。人気SFストーリー。
【初級】
1,600 円（本体価格）
四六判変形 168 ページ
【978-4-89407-499-6】

パパが遺した物語　iPen対応

ニューヨークを舞台に孤独なヒロインの苦悩と作家の父との絆を描いたヒューマンドラマ。
【中級】
1,600 円（本体価格）
四六判変形 152 ページ
【978-4-89407-553-5】

陽のあたる場所　iPen対応
叔父の工場で働く青年は、禁止されている社内恋愛を始めるが、上流階級の令嬢ともつきあうことに。果たして、彼が選ぶのは…。
【中級】
1,400 円（本体価格）
四六判変形 152 ページ
【978-4-89407-530-6】

ヒューゴの不思議な発明　iPen対応

駅の時計台に一人で住むヒューゴ。父の遺品である機械人形に導かれ、映画監督の過去を隠す老人の人生を蘇らせる。
【中級】
1,600 円（本体価格）
四六判変形 160 ページ
【978-4-89407-535-1】

プラダを着た悪魔 再改訂版

ジャーナリスト志望のアンディが、一流ファッション誌の編集長ミランダのアシスタントとなった…。
【中級】
1,600 円（本体価格）
四六判変形 200 ページ
【978-4-89407-587-0】

フリーダム・ライターズ　iPen対応

ロサンゼルスの人種間の対立が激しい高校で、新任教師が生徒に生きる希望を与えようと奮闘する、感動の実話。
【上級】
1,600 円（本体価格）
四六判変形 184 ページ
【978-4-89407-474-3】

ラブ・アクチュアリー　iPen対応

人恋しくなるクリスマスの時期に、様々な関係の10組の人々から浮かび上がるそれぞれの「愛」のかたち。
【中級】
1,600 円（本体価格）
四六判変形 192 ページ
【978-4-89407-558-0】

ローマの休日　iPen対応

王女アンは、過密スケジュールに嫌気がさし、ローマ市街に抜け出す。A・ヘプバーン主演の名作。
【中級】
1,400 円（本体価格）
四六判変形 200 ページ
【978-4-89407-467-5】

Business English in Movies　iPen対応

映画史に残る名シーンから、ビジネス用語をテーマ別、場面別に幅広く学べます。
鶴岡　公幸／Matthew Wilson／早川　知子　共著
B5 判 160 ページ
1,600 円（本体価格）
【978-4-89407-518-4】

嵐が丘　DVD 付

荒涼とした館「嵐が丘」を舞台にしたヒースクリフとキャシーの愛憎の物語。
【中級】
1,500 円（本体価格）
四六判変形 168 ページ
【978-4-89407-455-2】

或る夜の出来事　DVD 付

ニューヨーク行きの夜行バスで出会った大富豪の娘としがない新聞記者の恋の結末は…。
【中級】
1,500 円（本体価格）
四六判変形 204 ページ
【978-4-89407-457-6】

イヴの総て　DVD 付

大女優マーゴを献身的に世話するイヴ。その裏には恐ろしい本性が隠されていた。
【中級】
1,500 円（本体価格）
四六判変形 248 ページ
【978-4-89407-436-1】

※ 2019 年 8 月現在

出版物のご案内 － 最新情報はホームページをご覧ください

失われた週末　DVD付

重度のアルコール依存症のドンは、何とか依存症を克服しようとするが…。
中級
1,500円(本体価格)
四六判変形 168ページ
【978-4-89407-463-7】

サンセット大通り　DVD付

サンセット大通りのある邸宅で死体が発見された…。その死体が語る事件の全容とは？
中級
1,500円(本体価格)
四六判変形 192ページ
【978-4-89407-461-3】

ナイアガラ　DVD付

ローズは、浮気相手と共謀し夫を事故に見せかけ殺害しようと企むが…。
中級
1,500円(本体価格)
四六判変形 136ページ
【978-4-89407-433-0】

欲望という名の電車　DVD付

50年代初頭のニューオリンズを舞台に「性と暴力」、「精神的な病」をテーマとした作品。
上級
1,500円(本体価格)
四六判変形 228ページ
【978-4-89407-459-0】

レベッカ　DVD付
後妻となった「私」は、次第にレベッカの見えない影に追い詰められていく…。
中級
1,500円(本体価格)
四六判変形 216ページ
【978-4-89407-464-4】

アイ・アム・サム

7歳程度の知能しか持たないサムは、娘のルーシーと幸せに暮らしていたが、ある日愛娘を児童福祉局に奪われてしまう。
中級
A5判 199ページ
【978-4-89407-300-5】

赤毛のアン

赤毛のおしゃべりな女の子、アンの日常はいつも騒動で溢れている。世界中で読み継がれる永遠の名作。
最上級
A5判 132ページ
【978-4-89407-143-8】

ウォルター少年と、夏の日

夏の間、大叔父の家で過ごすウォルター少年。退屈な田舎での夏休みが、老人ふたりの昔話から、魅惑に満ちた日々へと変わっていく。
中級
A5判 168ページ
【978-4-89407-367-8】

麗しのサブリナ

名匠ビリー・ワイルダーがメガホンを取り、大富豪の兄弟と、美しく変身したお抱え運転手の娘との恋を描く。
初級
A5判 120ページ
【978-4-89407-135-3】

カサブランカ

第2次大戦中、モロッコの港町カサブランカでカフェを営むリックの元に昔の恋人イルザが現れる。時代に翻弄される2人の運命は…。
中級
A5判 200ページ
【978-4-89407-419-4】

風と共に去りぬ

南北戦争前後の動乱期を不屈の精神で生き抜いた女性、スカーレット・オハラの半生を描く。
上級
1,800円(本体価格)
A5判 272ページ
【978-4-89407-422-4】

クリスティーナの好きなコト

クリスティーナは仕事も遊びもいつも全開。クラブで出会ったピーターに一目惚れするが…。女同士のはしゃぎまくりラブコメ。
上級
A5判 157ページ
【978-4-89407-325-8】

交渉人

映画『交渉人』を題材に、松本道弘氏が英語での交渉術を徹底解説。和英対訳完全セリフ集付き。
上級
1,800円(本体価格)
A5判 336ページ
【978-4-89407-302-9】

サンキュー・スモーキング

タバコ研究アカデミー広報部長のニックは巧みな話術とスマイルで業界のために戦うが、人生最大のピンチが彼を襲う！
上級
四六判変形 168ページ
【978-4-89407-437-8】

JUNO／ジュノ

ミネソタ州在住の16歳の女子高生ジュノは、同級生のポーリーと興味本位で一度だけしたセックスで妊娠してしまう。
上級
A5判 156ページ
【978-4-89407-420-0】

出版物のご案内　　　　　　　　　　価格表示のないものは 1,200 円（本体価格）

シンデレラマン

貧困の中、家族の幸せを願い、命を懸けて戦い抜いた男の半生を描く。実在のボクサー、ジム・ブラドックの奇跡の実話。

中級
A5 判 208 ページ
【978-4-89407-381-4】

スーパーサイズ・ミー

1日3食、1カ月間ファーストフードを食べ続けるとどうなる？ 最高で最悪な人体実験に挑むドキュメンタリー映画。

上級
A5 判 192 ページ
【978-4-89407-377-7】

スラムドッグ$ミリオネア

スラム育ちの少年ジャマールはクイズ番組で一攫千金、恋人との再会をはたす。なぜ彼はクイズの答えを知っていたのか。

上級
A5 判 168 ページ
【978-4-89407-428-6】

ダイ・ハード 4.0

全米のインフラ管理システムがハッキングされた。マクレーン警部補は史上最悪のサイバー・テロに巻き込まれていく…。

上級
A5 判 176 ページ
【978-4-89407-417-0】

ハート・ロッカー

米軍爆発物処理班の新リーダーとなったジェームズ二等軍曹は生死を懸けた任務の中、無謀な行動を続け…。

中級
四六判変形 188 ページ
【978-4-89407-453-8】

フィールド・オブ・ドリームス

アイオワ州で農業を営むレイは、ある日、天の声を聞く。以来、彼は、えも言われぬ不思議な力に導かれていくのであった。

中級
A5 判 96 ページ
【978-4-89407-082-0】

ミルク

アメリカで初めてゲイと公表し、公職についた男性ハーヴィー・ミルク。だが、その翌年最大の悲劇が彼を襲う…。

中級
四六判変形 192 ページ
【978-4-89407-435-4】

メイド・イン・マンハッタン

マンハッタンのホテルで客室係として働くマリー。ある日大統領候補のクリスが宿泊に来たことでラブストーリーが始まる。

中級
A5 判 168 ページ
【978-4-89407-338-8】

モナリザ・スマイル

名門大学に赴任したキャサリンは、教科書通りで完璧に振る舞う生徒達に、新しい時代の女性の生き方を問いかける。

中級
A5 判 200 ページ
【978-4-89407-362-3】

ロミオ&ジュリエット

互いの家族が対立し合うロミオとジュリエットは、許されぬ恋に落ちていく。ディカプリオが古典のリメイクに挑む野心作。

最上級
A5 判 171 ページ
【978-4-89407-213-8】

ワーキング・ガール

証券会社で働くテスは、学歴は無いが、人一倍旺盛な努力家。ある日、上司に企画提案を横取りされてしまい…。

中級
A5 判 104 ページ
【978-4-89407-081-3】

アメリカ映画の名セリフベスト 100

アメリカ映画100周年を記念して選ばれたセリフのオールタイムベスト！ 映画ファンも納得の情報量でお届けします！
曽根田憲三・實壽貴之 監修
A5 判 272 ページ
1,600 円（本体価格）
【978-4-89407-550-4】

イギリスを語る映画

イギリスを舞台にした30本の映画を取り上げ、スクリーンに何気なく映し出される光景から感じられる文化や歴史を解説。
三谷康之 著
B6 判 172 ページ
1,500 円（本体価格）
【978-4-89407-241-1】

映画英語教育のすすめ

英会話オーラル・コミュニケーション教育に「映画」を利用することが注目されています。全国の英語教師必読の書。
スクリーンプレイ編集部 著
B6 判 218 ページ
1,262 円（本体価格）
【978-4-89407-111-7】

映画英語授業デザイン集

「映画を使って英語を教えたい」または「学びたい」という人に必見。25種類の授業紹介とワークシートがついています。
ATEM東日本支部 監修
A5 判 176 ページ
1,800 円（本体価格）
【978-4-89407-472-9】

※ 2019年8月現在

出版物のご案内 ― 最新情報はホームページをご覧ください

映画（シナリオ）の書き方

いいシナリオには秘密があります。アカデミー賞受賞映画を分析し、優れた映画シナリオの書き方をお教えします。

新田 晴彦 著
A5 判 304 ページ
1,300 円（本体価格）
【978-4-89407-140-7】

映画で学ぶアメリカ大統領

国際政治学者である筆者が、11本もの大統領映画を通じてアメリカの大統領制や政治、社会の仕組みを解説します。

舛添 要一 著
B6 判変形 272 ページ
952 円（本体価格）
【978-4-89407-248-0】

映画の中の星条旗

アメリカの現代社会について100のテーマを選びそれについて関係の深い映画の場面を紹介・解説しています。

八尋 春海 編著
A5 判 240 ページ
1,500 円（本体価格）
【978-4-89407-399-9】

映画の中のマザーグース

176本の映画に見つけた、86編のマザーグース。英米人の心のふるさとを、映画の中に訪ねてみました。

鳥山 淳子 著
A5 判 258 ページ
1,300 円（本体価格）
【978-4-89407-142-1】

もっと知りたいマザーグース

『映画の中のマザーグース』に続く第2作。映画だけでなく文学、ポップス、漫画とジャンルを広げての紹介。

鳥山 淳子 著
A5 判 280 ページ
1,200 円（本体価格）
【978-4-89407-321-0】

英語でひもとく風と共に去りぬ

『風と共に去りぬ』のすべてがわかる「読む映画本」。世界中が感動した名セリフを英語と和訳で解説。裏話も紹介。

大井 龍 著
A5 判 184 ページ
1,200 円（本体価格）
【978-4-89407-358-6】

英語学習のための特選映画100選 小学生編

映画英語アカデミー学会（TAME）の先生20名が小学生向け映画100本を用いた授業方法を提案。

TAME 監修
B5 判 224 ページ
1,400 円（本体価格）
【978-4-89407-521-4】

英語学習のための特選映画100選 中学生編

映画英語アカデミー学会（TAME）の先生10名が中学生向け映画100本を用いた授業方法を提案。

TAME 監修
B5 判 224 ページ
1,400 円（本体価格）
【978-4-89407-540-5】

英語学習のための特選映画100選 高校生編

高校生の英語学習に役立つ映画を100本集めました。英語が楽しく学べる1冊です。

TAME 監修
B5 判 224 ページ
1,400 円（本体価格）
【978-4-89407-568-9】

英語学習のための特選映画100選 大学生編

英語学習に最適な映画の世代別オールタイムベスト！大学生だからこそ共感できる映画で英語を学ぼう。

TAME 監修
B5 判 224 ページ
1,400 円（本体価格）
【978-4-89407-551-1】

英語学習のための特選映画100選 社会人編

社会人が働きながら、即役立つ英語を効率よく習得するために最適な映画を業界別にしてご紹介！

TAME 監修
B5 判 224 ページ
1,400 円（本体価格）
【978-4-89407-569-6】

おもてなしの英語表現集

来日観光客を安心して迎えるための即戦力！多様な場面で役立つ5,000以上の会話表現を収録した総合表現集です。

曽根田 憲三 監修
四六判 480 ページ
1,800 円（本体価格）
【978-4-89407-596-2】

音読したい、映画の英語

声に出して読みたい映画の名セリフを、50の映画から厳選してピックアップ。

映画英語教育学会／関西支部 著
藤江 善之 監修
B6 判 224 ページ
1,200 円（本体価格）
【978-4-89407-375-3】

図解50の法則 口語英文法入門 再改訂版

洋楽の歌詞と洋画・海外ドラマの台詞を例示して、口語英語の規則性を体系化。すべての英語教師・英語学習者必読の書。

小林 敏彦 著
A5 判 210 ページ
1,600 円（本体価格）
【978-4-89407-572-6】

武士道と英語道

テストのスコアアップだけではない、いわば効果性に強い英語道のすべてを、武士道を通して解説。

松本 道弘 著
四六判変形 208 ページ
「サムライの秘密」DVD 付
3,800 円（本体価格）
【978-4-89407-379-1】

出版物のご案内

ムービー DE イングリッシュ

50本の映画から厳選した英語表現や、あらすじ、こぼれ話など、映画を使って楽しく学ぶためのエッセンスが満載。
窪田 守弘 著
B6判変形 296ページ
1,200円(本体価格)
【978-4-89407-251-0】

2012年 第1回映画英語アカデミー賞

外国語として英語を学ぶ、小・中・高・大学生を対象にした教育的価値を評価し、特選する、"映画賞"記念すべき第1弾。
TAME 監修
B5判 216ページ
1,600円(本体価格)
【978-4-89407-476-7】

2013年 第2回映画英語アカデミー賞

映画の外国語教育的価値を評価し、特選する、"映画賞"の第2弾。受賞作:『ヒューゴの不思議な発明』『おとなのけんか』他
TAME 監修
B5判 248ページ
1,600円(本体価格)
【978-4-89407-506-1】

2014年 第3回映画英語アカデミー賞

映画の外国語教育的価値を評価し、特選する、"映画賞"の第3弾。受賞作:『ライフ・オブ・パイ』『華麗なるギャツビー』他
TAME 監修
B5判 216ページ
1,600円(本体価格)
【978-4-89407-524-5】

2015年 第4回映画英語アカデミー賞

映画の外国語教育的価値を評価し、特選する、"映画賞"の第4弾。受賞作:『アナと雪の女王』『ダイアナ』他
TAME 監修
B5判 224ページ
1600円(本体価格)
【978-4-89407-545-0】

2016年 第5回映画英語アカデミー賞

映画の外国語教育的価値を評価し、特選する、"映画賞"の第5弾。受賞作:『アバウト・タイム』『プロミスト・ランド』他
TAME 監修
B5判 224ページ
1,600円(本体価格)
【978-4-89407-557-3】

2017年 第6回映画英語アカデミー賞

映画の外国語教育的価値を評価し、特選する、"映画賞"の第6弾。受賞作:『マイ・インターン』『アリスのままで』他
TAME 監修
B5判 112ページ
1,200円(本体価格)
【978-4-89407-575-7】

2018年 第7回映画英語アカデミー賞

映画の外国語教育的価値を評価し、特選する、"映画賞"の第7弾。受賞作:『モアナと伝説の海』『LION/ライオン』他
TAME 監修
A5判 224ページ
1,400円(本体価格)
【978-4-89407-592-4】

2019年 第8回映画英語アカデミー賞

映画の外国語教育的価値を評価し、特選する、"映画賞"の第8弾。受賞作:『ワンダー君は太陽』『グレイテスト・ショーマン』他
TAME 監修
A5判 256ページ
1,400円(本体価格)
【978-4-89407-599-3】

オードリー at Home

息子が語る女優オードリー・ヘップバーンが愛したものすべて。家族ならではの思い出が詰まったレシピや写真も必見!オードリー・ヘップバーンのファンにとって、また食べ物を愛する者にとっても、ぜひ手に取ってほしい愛情たっぷりの"おいしい"一冊をどうぞ召し上がりください。
ルカ・ドッティ 著
B5変形判264ページ
3,600円(本体価格)
【978-4-89407-552-8】

サウンド・オブ・ミュージック・ストーリー

映画公開50周年を記念して発売され、瞬く間に全米で話題となったベストセラーがついに日本上陸!『サウンド・オブ・ミュージック』にまつわるすべてが分かる究極のファンブック!感動の名シーンや撮影の合間のオフショット、50年後の出演者たちの再会シーンなどお宝写真も必見!
トム・サントピエトロ著
B5変形判360ページ
2,900円(本体価格)
【978-4-89407-567-2】

ゴースト ~天国からのささやき スピリチュアルガイド

全米を感動の渦に巻き込んでいるスピリチュアルドラマの公式ガイドブック。シーズン1からシーズン3までのエピソード内容を完全収録し、キャストやモデルとなった霊能力者へのインタビュー、製作の舞台裏、超常現象解説などを掲載したファン必読の一冊。
B5判変形 178ページ
2,800円(本体価格)
【978-4-89407-444-6】

グラディエーター

第73回アカデミー作品賞受賞作『グラディエーター』のメイキング写真集。200点以上の写真や絵コンテ、ラフ・スケッチ、コスチューム・スケッチ、セットの設計図、デジタル画像などのビジュアル素材に加え、製作陣への膨大なインタビューを掲載。
A4判変形 160ページ
2,800円(本体価格)
【978-4-89407-254-1】

※2019年8月現在

編著者

寶壺　貴之	Takayuki Hoko	岐阜聖徳学園大学 映画英語アカデミー学会会長
クレイグ・アラン・フォルカー	Craig Alan Volker	言語学博士

著　者

井土　康仁	Yasuhito Ido	藤田医科大学
中澤　大貴	Hiroki Nakazawa	
山田　優奈	Yuna Yamada	

THE LIVES AND TIMES OF MOVIE STARS
映画スターの人生とその活躍の日々 -再改訂版-

再改訂版　第1刷　2019年9月5日	
編著者	寶壺　貴之　　クレイグ・アラン・フォルカー
著　者	井土　康仁　　中澤　大貴　　山田　優奈
音　声	Mark Hill, Amy Newsome, Sheila Patton, Sylvia Likami
発行者	鈴木　雅夫
編集者	鈴木　誠
発行所	株式会社フォーイン　スクリーンプレイ事業部 〒464-0025　名古屋市千種区桜ヶ丘292 Screenplay Dept. of FOURIN, INC. Sakuragaoka 292, Chikusa-ku, Nagoya, Aichi, 464-0025, Japan 振替口座・00860-3-99759 ☎ 052-789-1255 (代表)　／　FAX:052-789-1254
写　真	名作映画完全セリフ集 "スクリーンプレイ・シリーズ" より
特　許	吉田健治／グリッドマーク株式会社 (ドット印刷)
印刷所	株式会社チューエツ
コード	ISBN978-4-89407-600-6

無断で複写、転載することを禁じます。乱丁、落丁本はお取り替えいたします。Printed in Japan